My Shot of Joy

A MIRACULOUS JOURNEY OF REDEEMING
A LOST MOTHER-DAUGHTER RELATIONSHIP

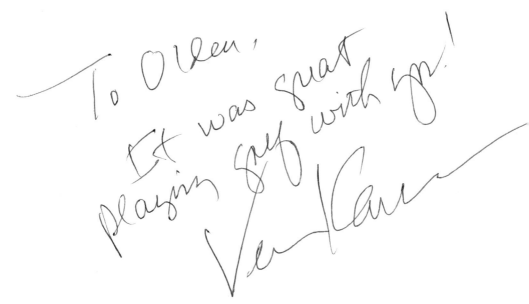

VERONICA KARAMAN

MY SHOT OF JOY
Copyright © 2016 by Veronica Karaman
True Champion Publishing

ISBN-13: 978-0692660850
ISBN-10: 0692660852

To all the estranged mothers and daughters who have a cry in their heart for the great divide to end and the miracle of a fresh start to begin. May you know the power of truth spoken in love to reconcile hearts, re-bond even the most impossible relationship, and re-create a lost legacy.

I dedicate my story to you. May you know there is a brand new story awaiting you now. May you know the power of love to heal mother-daughter relationships and to make all things new.

It's time for your shot of joy!

Veronica Karaman

Table of Contents

"The best shots are hit from the most impossible lies."
- Veronica Karaman

Introduction

I was in a race against time. My mother had just been diagnosed with a terminal heart condition and was given six months to live. Opting out of open heart surgery at the age of eighty-five, Mom had no other options for restoring her worn-out aortic valve. With the announcement that her time was quickly winding down, she was at peace with being at the end of her life. I, on the other hand, was not.

Mom and I had been emotionally estranged my entire life. There were many reasons for "the great divide" which kept us from having the blessed relationship we were meant to enjoy. Mom was a difficult person who just did not know how to connect with me.

In addition, we were decades apart in age, degrees apart in education, and light years away in how we viewed life. Golf was a big centerpiece to my entire life, starting from age five when my father first placed a putter in my hand and introduced me to the love of the game which continues even now at middle age. That span of time included winning national pee-wee putting contests, having a great amateur career as a teenager, and being the first girl from my high school to earn an athletic scholarship to college. After becoming a star golfer at Duke University, I played on the professional golf tour. My career highlight was playing in the 1989 Women's US Open. Mom thought the game was stupid! Help me, Jesus!

The great divide between us was only compounded by the death of my father at age fifty-nine. I was only fifteen when I lost him to cancer, and I didn't really know him, what made him tick.

I couldn't bear the thought of going through life without knowing at least one of my parents. I mean truly knowing them—their heart. My father's loss set up my twenty-five-year prayer: "God, please do not take Mommy until I know her. Please!"

When the alarm went off that Mom's time was short, I knew it was my season to reach her heart. I honestly did not know how it was going to happen, or if it could happen. But I did know that if my prayer was going to be answered, this was my one shot. I was either going to step up to the tee and take it, or forever not know if I could have hit it.

My personal stake was high. I had just received a full scholarship to earn my PhD in Leadership at Regent University and had started the program. I knew I couldn't focus on taking care of Mom and launching a rigorous educational track on top of trying to earn a living. I had also just purchased my first home and was dedicated to building my career. Get it—*my* career.

As I considered what it would take to reach Mom's heart and cross the great divide, I came to realize there were two great divides facing me. One was the relational one between Mom and me. The other was the one within myself.

The voices I kept hearing from my family members only magnified my challenge: "Let her go. Get on with your life. She has lived a good life. Now it's your time to live yours. Let her die. Move on." For months I struggled with what the pearl of great price was for me. Was it the advancement of my own personal life and career, which was finally in a place of momentum? Or was it to push the pause button on my life to focus on the one chance I had left to redeem a totally lost mother-daughter relationship? Was I going to give God the open space to work a miracle, knowing what little time she was given to live? What truly was the pearl of great price?

After months of deep consideration and much turmoil, I decided to listen to the voice within. I decided to relinquish my scholarship, suspend my personal plans, and give Mom my full focus. In doing so, I decided to step up to the tee and take my shot at life.

In addition to my faith, the one confidence I had to take the shot was in my lifelong experience as a competitive athlete. I knew how to prepare for and play in a championship. I knew that you never enter a championship with any other attitude than a resolve to win. You may not win, but you never enter a championship with any other belief, if indeed you want a chance at victory.

What I didn't realize until I faced both my great divides is that a championship is not reserved for only elite athletes, making all others mere spectators. Everybody has a championship. It can be attained by anyone who has a vision he or she wants to realize. For the first time, I came to understand that all my years of playing championships in competitive golf, including the US Open, would come to serve a higher purpose—an even more meaningful win than any victory I scored on the course. That championship would be redeeming my lost mother-daughter relationship.

My trophy would be coming to know Mom's heart and who she really was as her true self before she passed. My joy of victory would be to have the hole in my heart filled with my mother's love for me, and mine for her. It would also be the cherished memories that I missed growing up and that I would create to last the rest of my life.

Resolved to reconcile my relationship with my mother, I began my journey of redemption with a solemn declaration of commitment to victory from within: "I *will* reach your heart before you die. I do not care what it costs, what it takes, or how long it takes. *Whatever it takes* is my commitment to you—and to myself."

With this declaration, I stepped up to the tee and hit the most amazing shot of my life. Our relationship was totally redeemed, and Mom's six-month death sentence was extended almost seven more years! I collected enough memories to last a lifetime.

Some six years after Mom passed, I am now writing this story. Since then, I've shared the insights and strategies I learned with many others. As a result, hundreds of people have hit their own "shots of joy" and reclaimed lost relationships with their loved ones—mothers and daughters, mothers and sons, husbands and wives, brothers and sisters, stepdaughters and stepfathers, many times in a very short period of time. I never knew my own personal struggle and conquest would so powerfully help others.

As I have shared my story and offered workshops, seminars, and keynotes, I've discovered a universal truth: the cry of every human heart is for reconciliation of broken relationships. The need for deep human connection with loved ones is universal and a fundamental part of the human condition.

I decided to share my journey of redemption with you as a story. As a teacher and mentor, it's always my desire to train, coach, and equip. But instead of writing this book as an instructional guide, I'm trusting in the power of storytelling to inspire and empower you, my dear friend, in your own journey. My desire is for you to take courage, receive insight, and experience fresh hope to reclaim your lost or estranged relationship—and to know it is entirely possible. Most of all, I am writing this story to encourage you not to ignore your moment when the time comes to make a decision about your relationship with your loved one, who soon may be gone. So many people shrink back when the moment comes to make that heart-to-heart connection. In sports, the opportunity to hit a great shot most often presents itself when you are under pressure. The same holds true for life.

Champions are those who can perform under pressure. May my story help release the champion within you to cross your great divide and claim the victory of reaching your loved one's heart, for there is no victory if you quit. May my story inspire you to press forward with courage and not shrink back, to choose the pearl of great price, and to take the steps towards reconciliation.

As a trophy is the tangible evidence of a champion's victory, I begin my miraculous story with my perfect day with my mother.

A Perfect Day
with My Mother

It isn't often a mother and daughter share a perfect day together. The Reindeer Fun Run, held in early December 2007, was as close as it got for Mom and me.

The air was cold as I put on my doubled-lined sweater and prepared for my early morning race. What was special about this morning's inaugural race in Southern Pines was that you could run in it with your dog. Teddy-boy, our dog, was an American Eskimo. I was excited to decorate his all-white coat for the event, face-painting him with some green and red stripes. He looked like the official Christmas dog.

As easy as it was for me to get ready, Mom in her fragile health was much more of a challenge. I knew her time was short as she was nearing the end of her race at nine-one. A few weeks before, she'd had some flare-ups with congestive heart failure, and the

11

problem only exacerbated her aortic stenosis—a terminal heart condition. Her breathing was shallow; her heart was shutting down. Contemplating the doctor's determination that she had only about six weeks to live, I questioned the decision we had made by faith the day before, to venture out just as we had done so many other times. Should I take her to the race or leave her home? As careful as we needed to be about her health, her spirit was strong and vibrant. After all, everything about this morning's event reflected what her life and our relationship was all about: family, the dog, fun, the small town atmosphere, and running a race!

After I helped Mom get ready, we headed out the door. "I used to run everywhere," she proudly said as we drove to the race. "I would run to school and run home. I just loved to run."

"I know, Mom," I replied, finally realizing why just a year ago, at ninety, she had to walk to the grocery store and back, carrying her groceries all the way home, despite the doctor's strict orders not to do anything that would put stress on her heart. She was an athlete. That was her wiring. "That's why I bought you those pink Nike tennis shoes you're wearing. I wanted to see you run all the way to your finish line."

Mom continued, "I used to like basketball, too. But one day my stepfather made me quit playing the game because it scuffed up my one pair of shoes. Back then in the Depression we had it hard, and he wanted to be sure those shoes lasted."

"That's exactly why I bought you those shoes several years ago," I explained. "I wanted you to know that it was finally time for you to run free—and be the athlete you were always meant to be, even in your eighties. Those shoes represented a fresh start for you."

We both laughed over those pink Nike tennis shoes. She looked so "with it" despite her age and condition. I wasn't sure how much of the race Mom could actually enjoy or participate in. I did know she would gain much pleasure just from being in a competitive environment and watching her dog run. One of the greatest pleasures we had together was watching Teddy-boy run at full speed. He would run lightning fast with a big doggy smile on his face. Mom would be smiling just as big. Here was a chance for her to watch us run together in a holiday event designed for family fun.

We arrived at Broad Street early, before the crowd showed up. We discovered a parking space right in front of the park where the race would begin. It was a good place for Mom to view all the action.

Mom felt strong enough to venture outside for a few minutes. Finding a good perch on the bench, I could tell she enjoyed the view before her. The scene was the essence of small-town community: kids getting excited, moms and dads preparing for the race, the joy of being outdoors and engaging in sport—particularly in a race—everyone chuckling at the variety of dogs in their Christmas outfits, the camaraderie of neighbors. Every now and then a kid would stroll by our perch, point at Teddy-boy and remark, "Mommy, look at the green dog!" It was about as good as it could get for us. Although the air was cold, it was a perfect morning.

When it was time for the race to start, I gave Mom a kiss and headed to the starting line. She promised she would walk up to the starting line shortly after I got there to see me off, if she could.

"On your mark . . ." As the announcer spoke, I looked back to see Mom. I couldn't find her anywhere near the starting line. "Get set . . ." Was she able to get out of the car? My heart pounded as I realized this was the first time she was unable to walk more than fifty yards. "Go!" I had to trust that she was in the car and okay. My heart raced with joy and sadness as Teddy and I took off. Mom was with us, but right now it would be only in spirit. It was a strange feeling to take off without her in sight. I was moving forward while Mom was moving backward, both engaged in the race in very different movements.

As we rounded the last leg, I was slowing down. The ladies in front of me kept turning around and shouting to themselves, "We have to stay ahead of the green dog." Santa Claus and his elves were right behind me.

I repeatedly called out to Teddy-boy, "We have to stay ahead of Santa Claus!" My claim to fame is that I actually finished the race jogging most of the way. I looked for Mom and found her in the car.

"I tried walking up to the starting line, but I just didn't have enough wind in me. I came back to sit in the car," she said.

"I had a great race," I replied as I gave her a big kiss and the spear of reality pierced my heart. *Mom is shutting down.*

"I tell you what, Mom. Now that the race is over, let's drive up to the finish line." With everyone gone by then, I parked the car right in front of the line and helped her out. "Now raise your hands as you go through the arch!" Mom thrust up her arms in a cheer of victory as she paced through the finish line in her bright pink Nike tennis shoes. I caught a great picture of her with the word FINISH emblazoned right over her head on the big gray arch. It was as if she really was in the race with us, and at the same time, finishing up the race of her life.

Afterward, we headed to Lu's house. Lu was an elderly lady I thought might be a good friend to Mom. Again, I was torn between the need to face the inevitable, given the uncertainty of her survival, and the pull of faith that said, "Keep helping her to live life each day." Lu was possibly looking for a roommate, and although I didn't think it would be the right situation for Mom, I figured it would be worth it for the two of them to meet.

After our initial greeting, I just sat in the chair and watched Mom engage in a lively conversation with Lu. It was if I was suspended from the conversation, not even there, sitting back and observing Mom present herself in a way that made me so proud of her.

While she always complained about her lack of education and a sense of inadequacy she had felt her whole life, there—right before my eyes—I was watching Mom carry off a brilliant conversation. I marveled at her poise as she sat up in her chair, her back straight, laughing and talking as if nothing at all was wrong with her.

Lu's sister, Karen, stopped by for a few minutes to chat. One of her first questions to Mom was, "Well, how old are you?"

"I'm ninety-one years old!" Mom exclaimed. The look of shock on Karen's face was a showstopper.

"You're not ninety-one! I can't believe it. How do you take care of your skin?" Mom had beautiful, smooth skin with few wrinkles. People often marveled at how radiant and supple her skin looked. Karen looked at my mother as if begging for the inside scoop on the latest beauty cream.

Without hesitation, Mom replied, "Hard work!" We all chuckled.

As I continued to watch Mom and Lu engage in "the good old days" talk, what all was wrong with their body parts, and insights about their various joys and pains, all I kept observing were my mother's excellent qualities: her extreme beauty, great intelligence despite not having more than a grade school education, a sharp wit, an inner strength produced by the very Depression I hated so much, and a flair for lively conversation. "Now there's an amazing woman," I thought to myself, as I observed her in a glorified state. She was revealing the true champion that she was and that I yearned to see my whole life. In that moment of insight, I saw that Mom was everything I had hoped to be, and I was deeply proud of who she had become. As in golf when you hit a pure shot, you not only feel it—you hear it, enjoy it, and are always surprised by the sheer fluidity of all your body parts working together to produce that hoped for, though not always realized, perfection. I had just observed a pure shot of my mother.

After about an hour at Lu's, we decided to grab some lunch at Nature's Own, my favorite organic food store. The store also has a small section where you can sit and eat a good lunch at a reasonable price. As we sat and enjoyed a small bowl of soup, Mom decided to get up and stroll around the store. Because of her allegiance to Food Lion, I was a bit surprised she was interested in shopping at a rather high-end organic food store, but the food-shopaholic in her could not help herself.

Having a moment to myself, I reached over to the bookcase in front of me. I grabbed a book by one of my favorite authors, Dr. Kathleen Northrop. *Mother-Daughter Wisdom* was a big, comprehensive book on the effect a woman's relationship with her mother has on her life. I had first read Northrop's book on menopause that outlined how a lack of nurture from our mothers can affect our health. She was the first person who tied together medicine, emotions, and spirituality to explain dysfunction and a path to wellness. She was the one who helped me to realize that much of my own illness through my adult years was due to a lack of nurture from my mother. I was now experiencing the fruit of forgiveness and my champion commitment to reverse that plight.

I began flipping the pages, thinking what a good read this would be. Then Mom came back at the table. "You're not going to buy *that* book are you?" That one question summarized the downside of our relationship: the squelching of my own freedom of choice and a cascading condemnation flowing down from the spirit behind her question which denounced spending money on anything that wasn't a bargain. To me it was a worthwhile investment, a great read on my continuing journey to wholeness as a woman. Do I buy the book or don't I?

There was a time when I would have sent the condescension

right back to her with a defiant, "I'll buy this book if I want to!" Over the course of time, however, I learned to choose my battles. "Yes, I will buy this book if I want to," I asserted to myself inwardly. "I'm my own person, freed from the ill effects of your Depression scars." I further affirmed myself by thinking, "I'll just come back another time to buy the book." So, proud of myself for affirming my own personhood without having the need to be outwardly combative, I picked up the check. "C'mon, Mom, let's go."

On the way home, she wanted to stop at Food Lion, her daily stop. As I strolled the aisles with her, I thought, "Why does she have to come to Food Lion every day? What's the deal?" And then it hit me. "This is the only place she can come to where she still has the power of choice. So much has been taken away from her because of her condition. At least at Food Lion, she can still exert control over her own life." Satisfied with my new insight, we both happily went through the checkout line and then home.

Once home, I said to myself, "I just had a perfect day with my mother. We enjoyed a great time at the Reindeer Fun Run, being outside with Teddy-boy, the kids, their families and dogs, enjoyed a small town community in the spirit and décor of Christmas, went to meet a new friend, and had a delicious lunch. We topped it all off with a routine visit to Food Lion." I couldn't contain my joy. The day represented everything my mother's life of simplicity entailed, and I told her so. Mom smiled and agreed. We hugged and called it a day.

And what a day it was. Little did I know Mom's coming through the finish line at the race would be more than figurative. It would become a very real moment of closure to her life and our relationship. This was the last normal day I would spend with her—and it was a perfect day. The next day she suffered a heart attack and died three weeks later.

As I look back, I realize just how significant the impact of that day was for me. It represented the pinnacle of a lifelong journey to have a real relationship with my mother. It represented my trophy of arrival from the previous seven years of taking care of her and the closure of a God-appointed season to know her. It represented God's faithfulness to me, in a very real way, to answer my prayer that He would not spring a surprise on me in taking Mom. It was an advanced notice from heaven that all things have been wrapped up and that her time had come. It was a profoundly real end of a ninety-one-year-old race well run by my mother. It was an amazingly loving gesture from God to show me that I, too, had run well. Mom had reached her finish line on a day that will forever be etched in my mind as my perfect day with my mother. It was an exclamation mark from above that a lost relationship had now been fully restored.

What was also profound for me was the realization that the language I used with my mother in telling her I was going to run all the way to the finish line with her was more than metaphorical. God literally took us both all the way to the finish line together. We ended up our seven-year journey, and more accurately, our life journey together, with an actual race, the Reindeer Fun Run. We weren't a twosome in the run. We were a threesome, being divinely guided by our Master Coach from above. Even more, having had our last normal day together at that memorable Reindeer Fun Run, I had to think that in a way, we were part of every family's race. Our relational dynamics were representative of the needs and desires of every family to be close, to bond, and to reconcile.

Reflecting on that day, I now also realize that the setup for my perfect day didn't just begin with a single decision made in advance of whether "to go or not to go" to the event. Rather, it had begun seven years before with some heart-wrenching, sleepless, and turbulent deliberations in the middle of the night to turn my heart toward my estranged mother.

When the Seasons Change

*M*y deliberations to turn my heart towards my mother in the last season of her life were rooted in a history of interpersonal conflict, emotional separation, loss, and a deep inner cry from my empty soul to connect with the most foundational relationship in my life before it was too late.

For twenty-five years I prayed to God to know my mother. My father died when I was fifteen after a brief bout with cancer. I didn't really know him. It wasn't as if he wasn't present in the house. He was a workaholic. He was present in his work, but he wasn't involved in my life. I didn't know him on an emotional level. In many ways, we were strangers in the house.

Mom was a workaholic, too. Although she didn't work outside of the home, she too, was uninvolved in my life at any deep emotional level. I remember one particular day when I wanted badly for her to play with me.

Her excuse was, "I'm ironing sheets. I'm busy!"

"Ironing sheets? Who cares about ironing sheets?" I said to myself. "It doesn't matter to me if my sheets are ironed or not. I want to spend some time with my mother!" My response to her constant unavailability was to see if I could make her miss me. I cooked up a plan to go bike riding all day long and stay away from the house for as long as I could. After sitting under a tree for a few hours, worn out from the ride, I just knew Mom would be looking for me, wondering where I was.

Once I got back at home, I asked her, "Did you miss me?"

"I didn't even know you were gone," she replied. My heart sank. That instance is profoundly representative of the separation that existed between Mom and me. In fact, as I write this, I can't think of even one instance growing up of when my mother played with me. I have no fond memories of experiences shared with her during my formative years.

The emotional alienation was only compounded by the huge generation gap that existed between us. Mom was in her early forties when I was born. Growing up, I not only had one generation gap to deal with, but two. The three dollar dress I wanted to buy, she refused to buy. It wasn't too extravagant for her to take the pattern off the store-bought dress and then make an exact replica of it herself. This bothered me because as a young girl, I wanted the pleasure of owning a store-bought dress.

Educationally, we were worlds apart. I earned three advanced degrees. Mom never made it past the sixth grade. The very penny she would save, I would gladly toss away. We never had any heart-to-heart talks growing up. One time in the seventh grade I got drunk at my friend Pam's house and acted out of control. The next morning her mother called me into her room, sat me down on a couch, and had a heart-to-heart talk with me. That was the first time in my life an authority figure had a meaningful parenting conversation with me. I went home thinking, "Why doesn't my mother ever talk to me like that?"

As I grew up, left home, went to college, and began to build a life, the gap between Mom and me only widened. I pursued a career in professional golf. Mom thought the game was stupid. Of course, if it wasn't related to work and suffering, it wasn't worthwhile for her.

As much as I couldn't relate to my mother and as far apart as our lives would become, I always yearned for a real relationship with her. For most of my life, it seemed like the tide had gone out. However, when Mom turned eighty-five, and it was time for me to consider taking care of her, the tide came back in.

It's almost as if God, in His mercy and providence, sets up the changing of the seasons to compel us to consider a second chance. Some adult children beckon to the call to return to their parents to care for them. Others are consumed with other priorities. For me, I was so bereft of any kind of meaningful connection with my mother my entire life, I beckoned to the call.

The decision to take care of my aging mother as she entered the last season of her life wasn't without great emotional struggle, however. I think it was difficult for me to turn my heart and life toward Mom for reasons that go beyond conquering the great gulf that existed between us.

I had endless questions and deliberations over how and what to do. I'm convinced that nobody teaches us how to navigate through the really important things in life. When is the last time you aced a course in "doing death well"? Our American culture doesn't even consider death or helping someone to prepare for it as a meaningful or necessary facet of life.

My questions were practical: How do I prepare well for my mother's death? How do I reach out to her? To what extent should I be involved in her life? Should I move? If so, when? To what extent should I allow my own life to be disrupted? What should I do?

I struggled to hear the right voice. So many voices were speaking to me that I couldn't tell which one deserved my greatest attention.

There was the voice of a culture that places little value on the elderly: "Why care about the aged? Why are you paying attention to an old woman? There's no need to. You are giving up valuable time."

There was the voice of family and friends: "Just leave her alone. She's lived her life. Just let her die. There's nothing you can do about her health condition. That's it. Get on with your life."

There were my own conflicting voices: "You've had an impossible relationship with your mother your whole life. Do you want to get beat up one more time? What difference can it make now? She wasn't what you needed her to be. Why be there for her?"

The other voice cried out, "Your mom needs you. You're the only one who can reach her soul. She needs you to be the grown up one now. Make room in your heart and life NOW."

I suffered many sleepless nights. Feeling a deep inner turbulence, I didn't know if what I was feeling was God or an evil presence. I wanted to respond to the call, but I honestly didn't know who was calling.

I knew that my battle wasn't unique to my own journey. There were others I knew who were discerning and responding to the call.

Nancy was a friend who moved across the country to take care of her elderly mother. "I just felt like it was time to be with her," she told me. "I rented my house, sold some of my goods, just picked up and moved. I hope I made the right decision. It's been very hard."

Another friend, Paula, made the decision to move out of state to Florida to be with her aging parents for an indefinite amount of time. She felt compelled to spend time with her father during his last season. As she told me her plans, she burst out crying, "I am torn between the broken pieces of my heart, the wrongful ways I was treated growing up, the grief I have experienced with my siblings, and the deep desire I have to see my father through to eternity."

Her soul, like mine, was swirling somewhere between the tide of seasons past and the beckoning to reach beyond the deep divide to reconcile with a soon-to-be-gone elderly parent.

Like Nancy and Paula, I did respond to the call. Everything became perfectly clear to me one sleepless night when I heard the only voice I really needed to hear.

The Call to Love

*P*eople make life-changing decisions from many different places. For some, choices arise from a rational, practical consideration of things. For me, there was a deep tugging in my gut to wake up, listen, and respond at a level that was new and unfamiliar. The relationship between a mother and daughter is the most foundational on earth. No attachment is stronger between two human beings. There are things we know intuitively about each other. Our feelings of love and sometimes hate run deep. It was from this place that I felt a profound stirring in my heart.

Although I didn't know it at the time, I came to realize that the night pains and inner conflict I was feeling was the emotional cry from my own mother's heart. It's a mysterious thing, a reality I can't explain. I just know from the womb of my own soul that my mother was crying out for someone to hear her, respond to her, and love her. I felt the emotions she was feeling. Call it compassion. Call it God's way of having deep respond to deep. I can't explain it any more than that. I felt her spirit, her separation, her deep need for another human being to touch her at the most profound level. She was crying out to be loved, and God was hitting me over the head to wake up and pay attention.

Outwardly, the cry of her heart came as a death wish, expressed in her speech every day. "I am ready to die. I just know I will be going any day now. None of that matters because I won't be here soon."

Although she was eighty-five at the time, I also knew in my gut it wasn't time for her to go just yet. She still had some living to do. At the time she was living in her own apartment, attached to the other end of my brother's house. Emotionally isolated and lonely, I knew Mom desperately needed some social interaction. I tried to do what I could to help her plug into retirement groups there, but nothing really worked.

One night as I was in prayer, I heard a clear voice, one that ascended beyond all the rest, silencing them all: "I want you to love your mother."

I responded, "I love my mother. I call her, visit her, write her, pray for her."

The Voice came again. "I want you to love your mother."

I responded again, as if the Voice hadn't heard me. "I love my mother. I call her, write her, visit her, pray for her."

"Didn't I teach you what love is?" the Voice asked.

"Yes," I said. "Love is meeting someone at her point of need."

"What is her point of need?" the Voice inquired.

"She needs to be rescued," I said.

"Then rescue her."

I sat in stunned silence. I knew I did not have that kind of love within myself. Responding to the call to love would mean a radical life change for me. I had just bought my first house and was on a career track. A divine call to love my mother, which meant inviting her to come live with me, was not part of my five-year plan. Finding a husband was, but not tending to my aging mother.

"I don't have that kind of love, God!" I pondered the smallness of my heart in light of His immense love. "I know You have the capacity to love my mother." After much deliberation, I surrendered. "Okay, You will have to love Mom through me, because my heart is too small. But I will open up my heart and give You permission to fill it, stretch it, and grow in me a greater capacity to love."

What followed my surrender to the highest call to love was the most amazing journey of my life.

Angel in the Night

Soon after I purchased my first and only home in Chesapeake, Virginia, Mom came for an extended visit. I was thrilled to move into my own home. It was a beautiful townhouse. The wallpaper in the bathrooms was particularly attractive. Everything, including the sea-foam green rug, was exactly the way I wanted it to be: perfect!

The first day Mom came to live with me I got busy decorating my new home—and Mom decided to do her own decorating, too! Walking into the downstairs bathroom, the one with my favorite wallpaper, I noticed something stuck on the wall. Mom had taken take one of those round air fresheners, the kind with the sticky tabs on it, and plastered it at eye level right on top of my beautiful wallpaper.

All my excitement turned to explosive anger. I knew it! My mother couldn't just let me enjoy my first week in my house without doing something to mess things up! I stomped into the living room where she was reading the paper. "Mom! How could you do such a stupid thing?" I was livid. "You know better than that! Now I have a big hole in my wallpaper from pulling that air freshener off the wall."

She was shaken and started crying. At that point, I lost it. I thought, "She asked for it. I know she knew better." At the same time, I knew I had hurt her in my outburst of anger. Needing to vent, I grabbed the dog and stomped out of the house.

Hurrying to put as much distance as possible between myself and Mom's inexcusable deed, I felt I was losing my patience and sanity for what seemed like the thousandth time. She had just come to visit me but I'd already reached my end point. "What was I thinking when Mom and I talked about her coming to live with me? Was I out of my mind? We are generations apart and can't see eye to eye on anything. You've got help me God—and I mean NOW!"

When I needed to get a perspective on things, I often went on a walk with my dog. This time was no different. In fact, I was putting the heavenly realm on red alert. I needed some immediate, divine intervention.

My precious little American Eskimo Spitz is a total adventurer. Dashing out of the house, he was happy to embark upon an evening walk. Although we usually walked straight down the street to the end, he pulled me to a side street. Not wanting another tug of war, I submitted to his leading. I could tell he was anxious to break into a run. All I wanted was to walk and vent my frustrations over the impasse with my mother. Tears spilled down my face. I had to get an answer. Thinking it would help to talk out loud, I began voicing my frustrations to God as if He were right there walking by my side. "God, You have got to help me or I'm going to go crazy. I need an answer. I need You to speak to me now!"

Teddy kept pulling me down an unfamiliar street in my new neighborhood. As we passed the first cul-de-sac, Teddy spotted a lady standing in front of her house. Always up for attention, he quickly darted over to her. "Oh how cute. What a sweet boy!" the lady said from what seemed like a hundred yards away.

"How can she even see him?" I thought. "Must be dog person." Dragging me along, Teddy ran over to her, and she stooped down to pet him. Embarrassed, and with tears running down my face, I said, "Hi! Sorry for my tears. I just had a fight with my mother. I came out here to scream at God and release my frustration. I just can't seem to connect with her."

She somehow knew just what I was talking about. After giving me a hug, this total stranger opened up to me and spoke to my heart, "Oh, honey, let me tell you something. Both my mother and father died earlier this year. Listen, when they're gone, they're gone. The best advice I could give you is to just love your mother. Just go home and love your mother."

"Love her? What do you mean love my mother? I want to strangle her." I knew she was right. And I also knew that somehow my prayer had been answered, and my dog Teddy was my night angel who led me to my answer. I asked for a swing-thought, a guiding mindset to help me get the victory in my relationship with Mom, and I got it. What's more, it was just a repeat of the same command I'd heard before, the one that motivated me in the first place to invite her to live with me. I thanked this kind neighbor and headed home.

Once in the door, I went straight to Mom's room. She was in bed, but awake with her head under the sheets. Mustering up all the courage I could, I humbly said, "Mom, I'm sorry I made you upset at me. Please forgive me and I want you to know I love you." It was a totally new thing for me to humble myself and be responsible for my own behavior and attitudes. For some reason it took me a lot of courage to be that vulnerable with Mom.

Teddy jumped up on the bed and stuck his nose under Mom's sheets, pulling them down like he always did in the morning to give her his good-morning kiss. I could tell Mom was crying and didn't want me to see her tears. She pulled the covers back up over her head. This time both Teddy and I pulled down the sheets. I cracked a slight smile.

"I forgive you," Mom whispered. Pulling her so she could sit up, we hugged each other.

"Mom, we have an enemy, and it's not one another. I want to learn how to connect with you and I want us to have a good relationship." That was the first time I turned around the emotional split that had happened so often between us. In fact, it defined our relationship. But that night, I did something brand new. I reached out to Mom's heart and asked for forgiveness. And with that one big act of humility and transparency on my part, my journey of a thousand turnings of my heart to love my mother began.

Trajectories

*T*he word "trajectory" is a term used in golf to describe the arc of the ball's flight. Most beginners have a weak ball flight that either skims low to the ground with a vicious curve to the left or to the right. Other trajectories sail up in the air, quickly lose their force, and nose-dive to the ground. Some look like they go sailing high into the air, but like a reverse U, they turn around and quickly die.

Without question, Tiger Woods hits the most amazing trajectories I've ever seen. One time at the PGA in Maryland, I stood watching his drives launch off the tee like a missile.

His ball not only flew by everyone else's, it sailed over the back fence by at least thirty yards. Most landed on the roof of a house on the other side of the fence. His balls were clearly hit into another orbit. Everyone stood in a daze, utterly amazed at his power.

During one of his demonstrations at a Tiger Woods Foundation clinic, he stood on the tee and called each of his shots—one was "a low three wood." He took his club and hit a three wood about 250 yards off the tee—it looked like the ball sailed that far, getting only about ten feet in the air for the entire trajectory. It was stunning.

The most powerful trajectories are those that have a penetrating launch, sail up into the sky at an acute angle, reach their pinnacle, and then begin to come down. When you hit a good trajectory, you know you're penetrating the earth's atmosphere and getting the most out of your shot.

When it came to hitting the best trajectory with my mother, I didn't want a weak, non-penetrating shot. I wanted to hit the most powerful trajectory I could, making the greatest impact in her life. I began to understand that in order to hit a Tiger Woods trajectory, one that penetrated into another atmosphere, I had to focus on things of eternal significance.

This wasn't merely about a visit with my mother. This was about helping her to finish strong in the last season of her life. It was about reconciliation, ending the divide between us. It was about creating a relationship with her that I never had. I wanted to build lasting memories with her, ones that would help carry me through the rest of my life. I wanted memories that would provide a powerful trajectory of remembrance with no regrets.

One night while I was praying, I asked God, "What is this all about? If I'm going to subject myself to intermittent emotional torture, could you at least provide me with a reason to submit myself to this process?"

As I became very still, the Voice spoke to me loud and clear, so clear that it startled me: "You are preparing her for death."

At that moment, I realized for the first time just how important the end of life is to God. We live in a culture where we celebrate the beginning of life and milestones like marriage, but as I mentioned before, we really don't do very well with the end of life. Where so much of the spirit of the age is to discard the elderly and their importance because they don't seem to be too useful to society, God doesn't look at them that way.

He looks at it as preparing older folks for the next step in life, the leap into eternity. His desire, as I discerned it, is to bring completion to their lives and to reconcile what needs to be reconciled. But God also had in mind something that needed to be imparted to me. I didn't know what it was at the time—I only knew that the season was going to be just as significant to me as it was to her, and I wanted to get the treasure out of it all. But I needed to understand the eternal meaning behind my daily battle and determination to get to the gold. The words from the Voice shook me into a sober reality and into the high calling of being used to help usher into eternity the most important person in my life. That was a call I could surrender to and commit myself to enduring the process, however joyful or painful it would be.

In my case, I didn't think it would be a long time. To put it in simple terms, Mom's diagnosis of a severe aortic stenosis meant that her aortic valve was totally worn out. Worst case scenario, the doctors gave her six months to live, unless of course she had open heart surgery. She opted out of that, feeling that the operation would be too traumatic for her to endure. We both had peace about her decision.

Having made that choice, I told her that I was committed to seeing her through to the finish line, whatever it took. Together, we would live by faith, enter into the life that was still to be lived, and not shrink back. The courage to forge ahead together by faith was an agreement that would prove to be the bedrock of our great adventure to come.

Little did I know we would create a trajectory that would far eclipse anything Tiger Woods could launch into the earth's atmosphere. With my eye now focused on eternity and the things that really matter, we were setting up a shot that would keep climbing and penetrating not only into this earth's atmosphere, but straight into the orbit of everlasting life!

It all began with a trip to the driving range.

Put Another Ball Down!

*H*ow do you help an old person live out her best life? That was the question I asked myself every day. At first I thought if I bought Mom a dog, he would keep her good company. So that's what we did. We got Teddy-boy, our charming American Eskimo Spitz. He truly became her closest companion. However, there was still a hole in her emotional heart that even the best dog couldn't fill.

I tried taking her to old folks' homes, but everyone was too old for her. She had absolutely no interest in hanging out with people her own age. They were too boring! She refused to go to senior citizen centers, even though they offered fun activities.

I began to wonder if she was trying to make it difficult for me on purpose or if there really wasn't any hope in giving her a quality life.

One day out of desperation, I said, "Mom, I've had it! I'm so frustrated trying to help you enjoy your life. Nothing I do seems to work. I tell you what, put your tennis shoes on. We're going to the golf course!" My directive surprised even me. Totally unpremeditated, the thought just came flying out of my mouth. Much to my surprise, Mom complied.

Once at the golf course, I helped her out with her grip and stance. She placed a ball down and stepped back, then all of a sudden took a big waggle with her club. She even waggled her little derriere. "Mom! Where did you get that waggle?" I cracked a smile.

"That's the way the pros do it!" she replied.

"I don't waggle and I'm a pro. You didn't get that from watching me!" Then, suddenly, and with no instruction, Mom took a big backswing, making a perfect shoulder turn. With perfect rhythm and force, she swung down, striking the ball right in the sweet spot, and sent her eight iron shot sailing almost a hundred yards in the air.

In utter astonishment, I stood watching this athlete-held-captive, releasing her true potential for the first time in my life—and hers. "Mom, that was amazing!" I put another ball down. She proceeded with her pre-shot routine as if she had done it a thousand times. A few waggles with the club, a few waggles with her behind, a look down the fairway. Whack! Another perfect shot. We both stood stunned as we watched the little white ball go sailing through the air against the backdrop of a clear blue Carolina sky.

"Mom! That's amazing!" I exclaimed for the second time. "I thought I got it from Dad! Forty years later, I just realized I got my golf ability from you!" The first hidden treasure from my surrender and commitment to "love my mother" just blew out of the box—the discovery of a mutual athletic ability, a gift that I never knew until then, that my mother had passed down to me.

By now, this expired woman who was tired of life and saddened from being the only sibling left in her family, looked up at me with fresh fire in her eyes. I will never forget that breakthrough moment.

Not only did she send the ball sailing through the air with a strong trajectory, but she also spoke words that conveyed a new trajectory of hope and glee from her soul as she loudly commanded me, "Put another ball down!"

I quickly obeyed as she took another impressive and seasoned-looking windup on her backswing. Whack! A third one in a row. By this time, we both looked like we'd just won the lottery! Mom looked up at me with the most glorious expression of self-discovery and exclaimed, "That was really good!" The realization that she could learn a new skill at eight-five was a resurrection moment for her and a great joy for me.

In a surprising moment, we'd discovered more than her latent athletic ability. We had stepped into a place of shared equality, a perfect place of friendship—the golf course.

The very game she had considered stupid now became a place of pure connection for us. Perhaps now it really was possible to form a new relationship, not based on fixing the past or each other, but rather, on stepping into the sacred place of a shared experience that drew out our commonly-shared DNA. Mom and I were athletes. I had developed and pursued my ability to the ranks of a professional. She was never given the opportunity—or never took it—to pursue hers.

Even as I was jumping for joy over her new-found golf connection, I was saddened by knowing that Mom was a woman deprived of the chance to develop her talent. That would have never happened if she'd been born in my generation. Growing up in the Depression and having a stepfather who took away her one pair of shoes so they would last, my mother was left with the sealing of her unrealized fate. It made me angry to think she had to stop playing basketball because it would only shorten her shoe span.

I had to wonder, "What other undeveloped talents does Mom have? If nobody ever invested themselves in her, what would happen if I did? Could an old person bloom late in her life? If I took the time and energy to focus on releasing my mother's talent and ability in her life's last season, what would she become?" As a person of faith, I also had spiritual questions, "Can the power of the Gospel reach an old person? Can the same new life and vitality I have experienced through a personal relationship with God equally empower Mom at this waning stage of her life?"

As I pondered those questions, all of sudden, I had a new mission. It was not only to prepare Mom for death. It was to prepare her for life. I had to find out what other hidden treasures of human potential lay dormant within her. When reading the Scriptures one day, I came across a verse that became my guiding light and promise of "late-in-life fulfillment":

> The [uncompromisingly] righteous shall flourish like the palm tree [be long-lived, stately, upright, useful and fruitful]; they shall grow like a cedar in Lebanon [majestic, stable, durable, and incorruptible]. Planted in the house of the Lord, they shall flourish in the courts of our God. [Growing in grace] they shall still bring forth fruit in old age; they shall be full of sap [of spiritual vitality] and [rich in the] verdue of [trust, love, and contentment.] They are living memorials to show that the Lord is upright and faithful to His promises; He is my Rock and there is no unrighteousness in Him. (Psalm 92:12-15, Amplified)

What this said to me was that it was not God's will for old people to lose their spiritual vitality. There may be obvious limitations to what a person can do physically and even mentally, but she should still be bearing fruit. In other words, a person's soul should still be alive and well—not depressed and saddened, just existing—but actually advancing. I wondered what would happen if I clung to that verse by faith and began to apply it to Mom's life all the way to the finish line. If I partnered with God in a divine adventure to see what "flourish" would look like in Mom's life, I wondered what would transpire? I didn't know how long it would take to see the flourishing come to fruition, but I had to start, and I had to be committed to it all the way to the finish line.

Little did I know at the time that by my helping Mom to live her life to the fullest, it would also help me to live mine. The first spark of helping Mom to flourish occurred at the precise point of my own personal disappointment.

Teeing It Up Together

The year was 2001. It was a significant year, not only because it marked the beginning of Mom's golf career, but also because it marked a major downfall for me in my own golf career.

Just a year before, I had lamented to God that I despaired of life. At forty-one, I'd reached midlife with many of my goals unrealized. No husband. No family. No children. No flourishing career for myself.

One night I cried out to God, "If this is all my life is about, please take me. I don't want to live just existing. I need a desperate change of life."

A few weeks later, I received a call from Paul Newman's stunt man, Stan Barrett. Paul Newman was in his seventies at the time, so I had to wonder, "What kind of stunts is this guy doing for Newman, pushing his wheelchair?" Stan had called me on the recommendation of a mutual friend. He was a potential date, and I was open to meeting him.

After a few conversations, we decided to meet at the Washington Duke Hotel on the campus of Duke University. It was a familiar place for me, since I had attended college there.

What I found most fascinating about Stan was that he set the land speed record of going 750 miles per hour in a rocket-powered three-wheel vehicle! That was an amazing feat, and I knew that he had to be quite the "out of the box" person to do something like that.

My first impression of Stan was, "Hmmm . . . he resembles Paul a lot, but he's definitely too old for me!" After a lively two-hour discussion about faith, Stan turned to me and completely changed the subject. "So why did you quit golf?"

"Because I didn't have a swing that stands up under pressure, and having reached midlife, I wasn't making a living at it."

"Can others do the swing that you would like to have?" he probed.

I thought, "Who is this guy? I'm the one who is always challenging people, and now here is this guy challenging me." "Yes," I replied.

"Then you can do it," he insisted.

"You don't understand, " I continued. "I had great teachers like Jack Grout, Jack Nicklaus' teacher, and Peter Kostis, formerly with *Golf Digest* and now noted television commentator."

"No, *you* don't understand," Stan continued. "If others can do it, you can do it. If your teachers weren't able to help you, then you've had poor coaching."

For two whole hours Stan messed with my mind, challenging me to reconsider the decision I'd made to quit the game. "I just think there's something unresolved in your golf," he said, unwavering in his conviction as we finished up our four-hour dinner, heading to the car. As we said our goodbyes, he put his arm around me and prayed, "Father, don't let Veronica quit because of failure. Don't let that hold her back."

Driving home, I had to shake myself to know if what I had just experienced was real. I went to meet a man on a date and left challenged to reconsider my own sense of calling. For the next week, all I keep feeling on the inside were explosions of joy. I didn't know if they were for Stan or for golf! After much discernment, I realized they were for golf.

Taking a leap of faith to try one more time, I quickly secured some much-needed sponsorship monies and found myself playing competitive golf once again. My goal was to qualify for the 2001

Women's US Open to be held at Pine Needles, located in Southern Pines, North Carolina.

Although I made great progress in my game—having gone from shooting 80 to 69 in only six months after not playing competitively for years—I didn't qualify for the Women's Open that year. Heartbroken, I didn't know what to do. I had poured every ounce of my life and passion into the game with no world-class appearance to show for it. Perhaps my expectations were unrealistic in terms of the pace of my advancement, but nonetheless, I was deeply disappointed in the outcome of my all-out quest.

It was during this time that I first took Mom to the driving range. The timing was ironic because in a very real way, I was re-birthing my mother. In another way, Mom was about to re-birth me. Connecting to my mother through golf was the only thing that kept me in the game. I was so distraught from my unrealized dream of making the Open that I didn't care if I played again ever... until Mom and I took a trip to Pine Needles to play her first round of golf.

Mom's First Round

*D*uring a trip to play in a practice round for another golf tournament at Pine Needles, I decided to ask Mom to join me, along with my best friend, Peggy, who was also a novice at the game.

I loved Peggy because by her being a little older "best friend," she formed a nice cushion between Mom and me. She could relate to my generation as well as to Mom's. There were many times she would look at a conflict that had arisen between Mom and me, and reveal Mom's perspective on it. We were good enough friends that Peggy wasn't afraid to "tell me like it is" on any given subject. There were many times I was just plain mean to my mother in my responses, and Peggy would slap me upside my head and say, "Veronica, that was rude. You need to apologize to your mother." Other times she would say, "That was not very loving. You need to be nice to your mother."

Because I had great respect for Peggy's opinions, I could take hearing the truth from her, and it began to sink in that my mother was not the only difficult person in our relationship. I was!

So our trip to Pine Needles was a fun one, because the three of us enjoyed one another's company, and my mother felt very much at ease with Peggy as a mutual friend. When I was out of the loop in conversations about cooking, gardening, and "the good old days," Mom and Peggy found a connection that was impossible for Mom and me to enjoy. And that was fine with me.

However, on this day, we all teed it up together and were joined at the hip as we headed to the first tee at Pine Needles.

I'd always considered Pine Needles a special place because of Peggy Kirk Bell, the owner. A famed LPGA tour player and great teacher as well as one of the founding members of the LGPA (Ladies Professional Golf Association), Peggy was known for being a great ambassador to the game. Pine Needles always welcomed and honored women golfers. The Bell family also loved the Lord, so I took it as a special gift to the three of us for our complimentary round of golf.

As we approached the first tee, I noted Mom's appearance with admiration. She looked like a real golfer with her dark blue golf cap. She strode confidently up to the same tee marker that Annika Sorenstam had teed off from just a few months before at the US Open. She looked every bit the champion as Annika was. Mom grabbed her Patty Berg three wood, which was just about as old as she was, and took her characteristic waggle.

After a full windup on the backswing, Mom hit an absolutely perfect shot straight down the middle of the fairway. Both Peggy and I stood there for a moment, speechless, with our heads cocked and jaws wide open in utter astonishment. "Mom!" I exclaimed with great glee. "That was an amazing shot!" To see an eighty-five year old woman hit her first tee shot 150 yards straight down the center of the fairway at the famed Pine Needles Resort, site of the 2001 US Women's Open, was breathtaking.

"Hop in the cart, Mom. I'll drive you to your ball."

"No way, I'm not getting in any golf cart," she retorted. "I'm walking to my ball!" I laughed as she marched off the first tee. "Give me that club again," she commanded. "Just watch this one." After I helped her align her body to the target, Mom took another big backswing and proceeded to whiff the ball. "Look at that! I can't believe I missed the ball. After all that practice, I still can't get it right." We all chuckled again.

For the next six holes, Mom, Peggy, and I had an absolutely delightful time on the course, enjoying our good shots and bad.

The score didn't matter. All that mattered was that we were together, three great friends, having an unforgettable day on the course.

Here I was, the disheartened golf professional, teeing it up with an octogenarian first timer and grandmother to two children, along with a fifty-year old golfer. In what other game could such varied skill-leveled players come together in perfect harmony and equally enjoy one another's company? None but golf!

Both Mom and Peggy began to get tired as we approached the end of the front nine. Peggy and I had several more jaw-dropping looks of astonishment as we watched Mom hit many more strikes on the sweet spot. The long-awaited dormant ability of this aging athlete was beginning to be released. We both evidenced Mom's blossoming that day, and it was a great treasure to behold.

As we began our drive back that night, I couldn't help but think about the glory that had transpired that day. Here I was, ready to quit the game because I didn't perform to my own expectation and that of my sponsor earlier in the year. Here Mom was, ready to give up, too, because she didn't feel she had a reason to live. And here was a game, ready to be played by two women as far apart as the oceans could measure. As we frolicked down the fairways, our hearts were revived through the miracle of rare camaraderie and shared experience. Mom was re-birthing me in the game. I was re-birthing her. Peggy was our dear midwife.

God was giving us a gift of the game of golf. I was just beginning to understand the power within that gift to build relationships.

The Power of the Game

I had always been caught up on in seeing golf as a way to perfect a performance. Playing golf with Mom at Pine Needles was the first time I saw the beauty of the game to connect the hearts of people. This truth was driven home to me in a profound way. Earlier that year I had spent countless hours practicing, tens of thousands of dollars in tournament and other golf-related expenses, and much blood, sweat, and tears trying unsuccessfully to earn a certain kind of trophy. That trophy was one based on athletic ability, score, superior swinging, and besting my colleagues in heated competition of the highest kind. Although I'd made great progress in only six months, I lost. Based on a performance-oriented perspective, that made me a loser.

Playing golf with Mom, I began to see the sport in a whole new light. It wasn't about the score that day at Pine Needles. It was about the relationship and the way the game sets people in right relationship with one another naturally.

What I noticed was that as soon as Mom and I teed off, our focus was no longer on each other. Instead of criticizing and trying to change each other, we had a new focus that was completely outward. The target was something in front of us both—the golf course—and it was a common target we both could take dead aim at.

By keeping our eyes on the target, we were also able to walk down the fairway together. We could enjoy one another's company because we both had our own space and were acting responsibly for ourselves. Mom was making her own swings and was accountable for her own thoughts and actions. I was concentrating on my own game, although I was glad to be in her presence. We weren't trying to control each other, but rather granting each other the freedom to be completely our unique selves. We didn't have to try to do this. The game did it for us.

In golf you have to take total ownership of your own swing, and you alone are responsible for the results. You can't blame someone else for your bad shots. You alone take the credit for your good shots. Unlike team sports, you don't share the credit or blame for an outcome.

The independent nature of golf demands great self-awareness. To be a good player you have to develop body awareness, which means that you have to get in touch with yourself. For people who are used to putting blame on others or not taking responsibility for their own behaviors and attitudes, golf automatically requires that you take personal ownership of every thought, movement, and result.

As I began to look at the game as a way to connect with Mom, I wondered if playing golf could be used as a kind of teacher. If it was difficult for her to develop self-awareness off the golf course, could it be possible for her to develop it on the golf course? Could I then take the life lesson or discipline she learned from the game and help her translate that to her life? Could it be that God, in His goodness, had given us a common language through the game to begin to understand one another in a way we never had in our entire lives? I had to find out!

You Can't Change a Person, but You Can Change the Atmosphere

*G*olf was teaching me a life principle that I would experiment with over and over again each time Mom and I got together: you can't change a person, but you can change the atmosphere.

My fault in the journey to connect with my mother was that I originally thought subconsciously that if I could change my mother, it would be easier for me to have a relationship with her. What I learned from the day at Pine Needles was that I didn't have to change my mother to enjoy her company. All I had to do was get into the right atmosphere where we both could enjoy one another's company and have a shared experience.

There were many times I put into practice my theory of "relationship transformation" between Mom and me using golf as our "atmosphere changer."

One time Mom and I were arguing. Getting nowhere, I said in frustration, "Mom, let's just go to the golf course. Put on your pink Nike tennis shoes. Let's go tee it up."

Once we got to the course and took our eyes off each other, we started enjoying ourselves. It only took a few holes. Anger melted into enjoyment. Fear turned into laughter. Separation u-turned into connection.

One of my greatest challenges was for Mom to understand

how debilitating her negative spirit was. I came to realize this was a generational thing, but her negativity completely squelched my spirit to the point where I felt beat up all the time.

Once on the course, I helped her set up to her shot, then said, "Mom, do you see the hole? Envision hitting it right at the hole. Don't think about missing it. Think about hitting your target. You can do it! C'mon!" She looked at me in bewilderment. I knew I was challenging her mindset. For her to think positively was like asking her to fly to the moon. Being such a good student, however, she accepted the challenge. After taking her signature waggle of her clubhead, and then her behind, she made a full shoulder turn, and swung down fearlessly at the ball. To her utter amazement, the ball went sailing directly at the pin, landing about three feet from the hole!

Her eyes popped wide open. "I can't believe I did that!" she said. I could literally see the new tracks being laid down in her brain. I could tell she had lost the tracking in her brain to actually believe she could set her mind to accomplish something. She discovered that through positive thinking, she actually did accomplish it and stunned herself in the process.

Back home, Mom began to be negative again. This time I had a frame of reference for her, a fresh one from the course. "Mom, what you experienced today was the power of positive thinking. Right now you are thinking and acting negatively. Do you get it?"

"Yes," she replied sincerely.

"Okay, from now on, when you start going down this whole 'negativity trail,' I am going to invoke a 'negativity penalty.'"

"What's that?" Mom asked.

"It's a five dollar penalty you have to pay each time you get really negative." Mom smiled. She knew what I was talking about!

Another time, years later, I picked her up from her apartment in Fayetteville. I could tell she was feeling isolated and deeply discouraged. She needed to be with people and not just the television. Trying to talk to her didn't do any good. After I got her, we dropped off her suitcase at my house. I then executed my plan.

"Mom, get your putter. These wonderful children from all over the world are playing in a major championship at Pinehurst Resort this week. Let's go see them." Mom grabbed her putter and off we went.

When we started putting on the large putting green at Pinehurst Resort, we noticed two small Venezuelan boys putting nearby. They looked like two little Tiger Woods midgets. They couldn't have been more than nine years old, both sporting shoes that must have been size 10. Mom lit up. "Hey, where are you boys from?" she asked. Not sure whether these young champs answered her in English or not, she got a kick out of watching them practice, so she started putting with them.

It was as if Mom herself became a nine-year-old champ right along with them. Within thirty minutes of putting with the boys, she was her old self again. It was as if an invisible oxygen tank was filling her soul with fresh wind. Doing something that was so natural for her to do—that is, exercising her athletic muscles in a fresh and exciting atmosphere—brought her back into relationship and out of isolation. All it took was placing her into the atmosphere. Her depression turned to happiness, so after putting, we drove home, and everything was okay.

Somehow, the golf course became not only our teacher, but our emotional home, too. It was a healthy place of connection, which is what home is supposed to be about. Never once did Mom and I experience anything negative on the golf course. I desperately wanted to experience "being home with my mother." Unfortunately, the atmosphere of the home I grew up in was very different.

Creating a New Home

*H*enri Nouwen, in his classic book, *Life-signs: Intimacy, Ecstasy, and Fecundity in Christian Perspective*, talks about what home should be like. Home should be a place of intimacy, joy, and fruitfulness. It should be place where our soul finds a safe haven, a sanctuary in which to grow. Home should be a place of total and unconditional acceptance, where you feel you can be yourself, where all of you—the good parts and the bad parts—can find rest. It is also a place of truth, where someone can speak to you about becoming your best self without threat of separation or condemnation. It's where your life rubs against my life, and instead of beating one another up in that rub, we sharpen one another. Home should be a place where we are deeply known and where we can deeply know another person. That is what family is all about.

My home was not like that. It was not a place where I intimately knew my parents or my brother. Our family dynamics were about performance. For instance, one time I told my father that I had forgotten to say my prayers. He sternly looked at me and chastised me. In order to be the perfect little Catholic girl, I said my prayers twice that night to make up for the night I forgot. I learned that going to my father and confessing my faults was not a safe thing to do. The weak parts of my soul that needed affirmation and acceptance were met with judgment and condemnation.

It wasn't until much later that I realized just how tragic my home life was as an emotionally vacant place. I never experienced deep bonding with my parents. We lived more or less as four independent individuals in the same house, but never had any real connection. My parents never had any heart-to-heart talks with me. Even when my mom busted me for experimenting with drugs, she never "talked it through with me." She just said to stay away from the person who was a bad influence on my life. I yearned for a real relationship with my parents. Although I never had that with my dad, except for moments here and there, I was determined to create a bond with Mom.

Fast forward to Mom's and my new beginning. Somehow, our roles were reversing. Mom was becoming more like a child, and I, like her parent. As much as I disliked that strange relational dynamic, I knew that I was her only hope of creating a new sense of home between us.

The good news was that I discovered I had the creative power to change the atmosphere. Although I couldn't not fix the past, I could start something brand new. While my childhood home represented emotional vacancy, and my home in Chesapeake with Mom represented emotional violation, I could begin to create an environment of emotional connection.

One of the first times Mom and I connected "at home" was when I was living in Florida. I took a job there working at a college in 2003. Mom came to visit me for a period of time, and the emotional tug of war began again. We hadn't played golf together for some time, so the common ground we had gained was not immediately accessible.

While in deep angst one morning, I cried out to God again. "You've got to help me," I prayed. " I can't stand this beautiful home being a place of such negativity and strife. What do I do?"

I felt the Voice say to me, "The reason you are so frustrated is that you have not taken your place of authority in your home. You have allowed the negativity to exist. Take your authority." So I did.

The next morning I gently said to my mother, "Mom, I love you, but this is my house. And in my house, we are going to have peace. If you don't want that, okay. I can take you back to the airport tomorrow. If you do want that, then the only way I know how to have peace is to start our day off with prayer and reading the Bible."

"Well, I don't know if I like your rules," Mom shot back.

"These are not rules, but like I said, I can take you back to the airport if you don't want to respect my wishes."

The next morning Mom showed up at the breakfast table with me.

Every time we came together, I would sense the presence of God being with us. I know this, because after we read the Bible together and began to pray, Mom would cry. This was a total surprise to me.

One morning, out of the blue, she confessed, "I never knew my father." This was literally the first time Mom had ever shared her heart with me. I was floored. Here was an eighty-seven year old woman getting in touch with an eighty-four year old pain that was still present. My heart went out to her.

"Mom, you do have a Father, and it's time you get to know Him. You have a heavenly Father, and He loves you. Would it be all right to hold you?"

With tears streaming down her face, Mom nodded yes. I bent down on my knees and wrapped my arms around her. We both cried together. Mom let me touch her pain. It was our first moment of emotional intimacy that I could remember in my entire life. Not even when my father died did my family grieve together. We bore the loss in painful isolation. In this rare moment with my mother, I came to understand that on an emotional level she was deeply injured. A child of the Depression, her whole life was about surviving and suffering. She had no idea of how to get in touch with her feelings.

But when it came to body awareness, Mom was very much in touch with herself, and it was the game of golf that opened up this new self-discovery. It also brought about a connection between us as fellow athletes. I knew she was a natural athlete because during a golf lesson she was able to immediately respond to a verbal command to move her body in a certain way. I was impressed with this because normally an old person lacks that degree of awareness. When I said, "Keep your left heel down on your backswing," Mom could do it on the first try. Most normal people can't do that on their twentieth try.

Emotions were different for Mom. As I said, she'd always had a hard time recognizing and sorting them out. That's why her emotional honesty with me that morning was such a huge gift, one that made all the mining of her soul worth every effort. I cherished that moment as an eternal one, the first of many to follow. I was glad I had set my aim at the farthest trajectory possible—one that would reach eternity. As much as golf produced joy and effortless connection with Mom as a fellow athlete, sharing her lifelong pain with me took courage more daunting than any of her impressive drives down the fairway.

When parents don't share their hearts in transparency and vulnerability with their children, it's impossible for their children to know them. I knew my mother and father as hard workers, even workaholics, but I did not know them intimately, what made them tick.

My loving encounter with Mom at the breakfast table was the first time I began to understand that there were reasons behind her aberrant and "difficult to get along with" behavior. She was a human being who had experienced horrific emotional struggles that were never healed.

Her very first memory was of her dead father being carried out of the house in a black bag when she was three years old. He died in the 1919 flu breakout. At the time, Mom was also very ill, and her mother thought she would die and her husband would live. Instead, Mom survived and her father didn't. Although my dad died when I was a teenager, at least I knew him. I couldn't imagine what it would be like to grow up totally fatherless. Mom's opening up her heart to me was a huge step in my extending compassion to her. I was pleased that I was also cultivating a listening ear to my heavenly Father who had told me to "set the bar" and refuse to allow strife to be the dominating force in my home.

Yet there was still strife within my own heart I had to deal with.

The Pearl of Great Price

*W*hen my job in Florida ended, I moved back to Virginia Beach. During that time, I received a $40,000 scholarship to pursue a PhD in Leadership Studies. Always believing that earning a doctorate was in my destiny, I thought this was it.

However, my heart was torn between dedicating an extra forty hours a week of my life to a particular program that I didn't have peace about, and continuing my PhD in "Studies of the Heart with Mom." Always being an intellect, I thought I was sabotaging my own career to continue caring for Mom. I fought an intense inner battle of the soul to determine what the pearl of great price really was for me. Was it to advance my academic career, or was it to continue to tend to my aging mother?

The world does not hand out gold stars for doing the most important things. They hand out accolades for achievement, not fulfillment, for accomplishment, not caring. Was I going to listen to the world's call or to the cry of my heart to experience full reconciliation—and restoration—with my mother? What price was I willing to pay? Giving this up would be a big one. There was no way I could do both. I didn't have that kind of energy. As much as Mom was having to be courageous to begin to open up her heart, I, too, had to make courageous decisions to pursue the cry of my own heart to know my mother.

I stayed in the PhD program for just a short while. The

intellectual stimulation I experienced during that brief period was exhilarating. I felt the synapses of my brain being ignited once again. To be affirmed by my professors and to feel part of a group of colleagues was food to my hungry soul. There was another part of my soul that was starving, too, and I was committed to keeping my promise to Mom to see her through—and to see how God would work a complete reconciliation between us.

When I opted out of the PhD program, several friends told me about a coaching program they thought would suit me well. One of the professors from the school had undergone a transformational experience during a talk with a fellow leader, which led him to dedicate his life to helping people grow. "The conversation is the relationship," he would often say. That line struck my heart because our family had had very little meaningful conversation during my growing up years. Without conversation, a relationship does not exist.

I knew this was a weak area in my life. I knew how to achieve things, set goals, and be determined. What I was not very good at was building healthy relationships with people.

Perhaps the life-coaching program and certification could more than equip me professionally. Perhaps it could help me personally to grow and heal myself, so I joined the program. The tools I learned in the Life-forming Leadership Coaching courses changed my life. To use a golf metaphor, they would also be the "relationship clubs" that would unlock the deep things of Mom's heart and unrealized potential.

New Kind of Tools

"*A* wise woman builds her house. A foolish one tears it down with her own hands." One morning as I was meditating on this verse, Proverbs 14:1, it struck me that I was using tools that tore down rather than built up a relationship with my mother.

I have some really old clubs in my golf bag, but they work for me. My sand wedge, which was my father's old Lynx club, I've had since I was fourteen years old. The "S" on the club is almost nonexistent. I keep using it because it still performs beautifully. I know this club intimately and it knows me. We've been together for so long that I consider it an extension of my arm. Perhaps there's a newer model that would work better, but I have confidence with this club. It gets the job done when I have to hit a high lob shot about seventy yards out and land softly on the green. I can hit a low chip shot with it as well as just about any kind of sand shot. It produces great shots.

I also have a driver with a stiff shaft in it. In fact, it is too stiff. When I miss a drive, the tendency is for my shot to drift off to the right. It's not the right club for me. I needed a driver with a more flexible shaft. Last year I won a driver as a prize in a tournament. When I went to the fitter to get a club with the right flex and degree of loft, I found one that I could just pound away on. It produced a great ball flight for me, much better than the stiff-shafted driver I was using, so I put the new driver in my bag instead.

In teaching golf to women, I've noticed that many times their clubs are much too heavy for them. Their husbands have given them their old steel-shafted clubs, and they can hardly swing them. When I give them a light-flexed, graphite shafted-driver, all of a sudden they can produce some good clubhead speed and swing freely through their shot. The ball instantly goes whizzing through the air, putting a big smile on their face!

So a good golf club can make all the difference in the world in your game, without changing your swing at all. Just as some clubs will add to your game and some will take away, I was learning that the same held true for relationships. Some "relationship tools" build your connection to another person, creating positive results. Others take away from your connection and actually tear it down, producing negative results.

In my relationship with Mom, I came to understand that I was using the wrong "clubs." As much as I wanted a positive connection with her, the tools I used were actually tearing down our friendship instead of building it up. Those negative, penalizing tools were criticism, judgmentalism, negativity, control, and anger. Every time I used those clubs, it sent our relationship ball-flight right into the heavy rough! I needed some new relationship clubs—and badly!

The first time I came in contact with positive relationship-building tools was in my life-coaching classes. It was a big adjustment for me to go to class and not be intellectually stimulated, but instead, to learn about matters of the heart between people. The instructors, Dr. Joseph Umidi and Tony Stolfus, spoke about these people-building and potential releasing tools as values.

As I continued through the courses, I wrote out my list of values, which became for me my new tools—my relationship clubs—to launch long-lasting, positive relationships:

1. Humility. I believe humility is the number one trait or tool for building a positive relationship. The opposite of pride, humility doesn't approach someone from a "top down" angle. Rather,

humility takes the low road. It doesn't expect people to live up to your standard. Nor is it commanding. It seeks to serve others, coming at them from where they are, not expecting them to rise to your level if they are not there. It is a "bottom-up" approach.

When I started to teach golf from an angle of humility, I found my students succeeding more quickly and at a higher level of competence than ever before. I wasn't coming to the lesson from a point of view of "this is what we are going to do today, and you better be ready to respond to my vision of your swing or else!"

Instead, I would approach the lesson by asking each student what he or she wanted to accomplish that day. I would then remove my agenda from the equation and simply seek to serve that person in the best way I knew how. I would take my students right where they were, with the sole objective of taking them to the next step.

I would have to discern what their capabilities were, what their mindset was for the day, and to what degree they possessed body awareness. I saw each person as a unique individual with her own pace of progress. Suddenly, my teaching was not about me as an instructor, but solely about releasing the skill and joy of my player. As my students left empowered, I began to see more and more the power of humility to reach them. They opened up to me because they knew I was loving them by meeting them right where they were.

2. Transparency. Transparency is simply the trait of being real. It's allowing people to see both your strong and weak sides. It's revealing who you truly are. If you're mad, it's having the courage to say, "I'm angry." If you're sad, transparency gives you the courage not to hide it. People open up to people who are real, especially today's youth. It doesn't matter how much you know. They want to know if you really care.

3. Responsibility. Taking personal responsibility for all my thoughts, actions, attitudes, and behaviors was a huge value leap for me. It was always easy for me to blame, give excuses, or deny

reality. In fact, I have observed that denial was a way of life in my family. There is a power to denial. It can keep you going and moving forward, but the fruit of it is not long-lasting. You have to deal with things, and if you want to grow, you have to take responsibility for yourself. There is no such word as "victim" in taking ownership of all your stuff.

4. The Power of Listening. One of the most effective tools I began to use and which achieved great results was the art of listening. Most of us are accustomed to telling people what we think. I learned in my coaching course that the number one reason conversations shut down is because of people giving unsolicited advice. People just don't like to be told what to do, unless of course, they ask for the information.

Paul Tillich wisely said, "The first duty of love is to listen." Listening is a skill that requires some finesse to cultivate, but anybody can do it. There are four levels:

a. Self-centered listening. This is when someone is talking and you are listening but not hearing, because the entire time you're thinking about something else. In golf terms, I call this "whiff listening."

b. Others-centered listening. In this second level of listening, you are tuned into what the other person is saying and not thinking about anything else. You're focused on the other person. In golf terms, I call this "solid contact listening."

c. Intuitive listening. In the third level of listening, you are tuned into what the other person is *not saying,* and you perceive what is going on with them emotionally or spiritually. Perhaps you become aware that they are afraid or shy or worried about something deeper. It's what you "pick up" about them at a deeper level.

d. Spiritual listening. I believe there is fourth level of listening, and that is hearing the voice of God. In listening to God, there is a voice that speaks to you when you become very still. It's not your voice, but One that impresses itself in your spirit and you know it is coming from God. This is the deepest level of listening.

Both intuitive listening and listening to God mean you are "hitting it dead perfect." I call this level of listening "hitting the sweet spot." When you hit the sweet spot in golf, it produces a pure sound, and you notice the difference in the sound immediately. When you are truly heard and truly hear someone, it produces a pure sound—one of peace, connection, understanding, and joy. You just know when you have connected with someone spirit to spirit.

5. Asking Powerful Questions. Cultivating the practice of asking powerful questions is by far the greatest tool I gained from my coach training. You can learn so much about a person from simply asking probing, sincere, and appropriate questions. Giving someone the space and freedom to express themselves is a great relationship building tool. Much information is gained from allowing the other person to come forward. I never coach or teach a person until I locate where they are. All effective coaching comes from discovering that emotional/spiritual location and then taking the person from that point to the next level. When you are truly interested in learning the interests, values, goals, dreams, concerns, and potential solutions of others, they feel incredibly valued.

6. Authenticity. Authenticity is the trait of being true to yourself. It incorporates both honesty and integrity. When you are being authentic, you are expressing your highest self and speaking from a place of connection to yourself. You can't connect with another person unless you have first connected with yourself and aren't trying to be someone you are not. Authenticity is the opposite of comparison and deceitfulness. It means having the courage to be who you are in the truest part of your identity. It means living from the core of who you are and not wavering from that place.

7. Intentionality. Being intentional means that things don't just happen. You have to make them happen. Just as in golf where you

have to be intentional about setting up your shot, so must you take aim at your relationships. If you want to hit a target, you have to pick one, set up to that target, and then go there! The same is true for relationships.

There are other coaching values I embraced, but the ones I've listed are what became the new building blocks to my life. In a sense, going into this coaching program was like buying a whole new set of clubs, guaranteed to produce great shots if I just practiced with the clubs using a good swing. Each shot I executed with my new relationship tool became more than just an individual shot. In the same way that each shot in golf is part of a larger round, each time I executed a relationship swing using my new tool, I was contributing to a transformational conversation.

The term "transformational conversation" is a coaching term that implies a conversation that makes a difference in your life. You come into the conversation one way, and as result of interacting with another person, you leave changed. My new relationship-building blocks helped me to connect with people at much deeper levels and experience connection much more quickly than before. I think the best conversations are those where you can speak spirit to spirit with someone.

What I learned through this program is that connecting with someone is not a matter of personality or chemistry, but of applying the principles of relationship building. Anyone can develop a substantive relationship with someone using the right building blocks.

As I was going through my coaching program, I was not only learning new tools to help me navigate more effectively through my relationship with Mom and others, I was also being healed myself. I felt my soul being nurtured. I felt like I was growing again.

At some point I must have passed some kind of test because right in the middle of my program, my Master Coach gave me the opportunity to put into practice everything I was learning with the challenge to take one big, daring leap.

One Big, Daring Leap

For twenty-five years I prayed, "Lord, don't take my mother until I know her." I wasn't sure how God was going to answer my prayer, but the moment finally arrived when I knew, "This is the season." It's funny how you can pray a fervent prayer but never really expect it to be answered. Such was my prayer. I think I prayed it out of total desperation, but when the season ordained for that prayer was to be answered, I was totally taken by surprise. Yes, I was delighted, but truly surprised.

I was in the middle of my coaching program when I needed to move. I was rooming with a friend at the time. However, I felt it was time to find another place since she was going through some major life changes herself. I thought of my mother and how she was to fit in with my moving plans. She and I had lived together in spurts. When she wasn't with me, she was back at her own place in Fayetteville, North Carolina. This was an apartment at the end of my brother, Mike's, house. As much as I wanted to connect with Mom, I realized we both needed our own space and that living together probably wasn't a good option. But maybe finding a place where she could visit for awhile as she had always done would work. Little did I know that behind the scenes, God was arranging a perfect plan for Mom and me. When she came to visit me in Virginia Beach over the Christmas holidays in 2004, we devoted a day to looking at rental homes.

We checked out a lovely little home down Bay Shore Drive towards the ocean, in the old money section of town called Bay Colony. We had a good interview with the owner, but as we drove away, I felt the Voice say clearly to me, "This is not the place for you."

"What!" I thought to myself. "Where is the place for me, then?"

As we drove a few blocks further, Mom and I spotted a "For Rent" sign in the corner lot of Bay Shore Drive and Cedar Point. The big grey house looked like it had been there for at least sixty years. "Let's stop, and check it out," Mom suggested. Her comment surprised me because up to this point she hadn't initiated our stopping to look at any house. I pulled in the gravel driveway. With hopes high, we got out of the car, walked up to the front of the house, and peeked in the windows.

It was a beautiful old home on about two acres of land with lots of trees and shrubs. With a huge back yard and large garage, it appeared to meet my needs. With two front doors, it appeared to meet more than my needs, as Mom seemed just as interested in the place as me. "Mom! Look over here. At this side of the house it looks like there's a space for a type of mother-in-law suite. You could live in this side of the house, and I could live on the other one. We could be together and both have our independence, too." The hardwood floors, arched doorways, and built-in bookcases piqued our interest.

"Call the landlord and see what the rent is," Mom said.

I had to drive her back to North Carolina later that day. On the way, we stopped at Burger King for lunch. Sitting across from each other, Mom looked at me and with laser-like perception said, "I can see you're dreaming about that house and have already moved in. And I can see myself scrubbing those floors." I looked at her completely dumbfounded. This was one of the rare times that we equally shared a vision and the only time Mom had initiated a comment so perceptive, it seemed she had read my mind.

"I can't believe what you just said, Mom. That's exactly what I was thinking. Are you telling me you see yourself living in that house, too?"

"Yes," she replied, "If the price is right." Up until that moment, I had been the one calling the shots with Mom. This was the one time she volunteered to join me out of her own desire. With a shared vision, I knew this was the right thing to do.

I called the owner. He gave me a great deal on the rent and agreed to let me move in on a short-term basis. A week later I moved into that house. It would be a place where Mom and I would build a deeper emotional connection. My brother had agreed to help pay some of the rent to cover Mom and move her furniture from North Carolina. The rental agreement was for six months to see if and how she and I could get along with one another. It was a huge risk, but one we both took. A month after I moved in, Mom joined me.

Everything up to this point in terms of our relationship was preparation, like practicing at the driving range or playing a casual round of golf. Now it was US Open time, and it required every ounce of our being to play the championship of our lives.

Growing the Soul in Winter

*M*oving into our new home together meant Mom and I would be sharing space equally for the first time. She was not moving into my home, as before. Nor was I visiting at her place, as I also had occasionally done. We were in this together, and I must admit, I didn't do a very good job for starters. Moving is a horrendously stressful activity, and the changes are always huge. Little did I know that Mom's moving at eighty-eight was too much of a change for her. The house on Cedar Point was fantastic, but old. You could feel a spirit of home, a sense of permanence and settlement from the people who had lived there before, obviously for a long time. There were problems with the heating system and water that only added to our stress. However, I knew this was our appointed time to be together. I had to find a way to get us connected, where we would experience the victory of deep relationship. But first, I had to see it in the invisible realm. A lesson from nature gave me hope.

My favorite room in the house was the Florida room. It was completely glassed in and served as a television room as well as a place to look out onto the beauty of the property. One morning I was observing all the dead foliage and wondering, "What plants and schrubs do I cut down and what do I leave alone?" Everything looked totally dead. I decided to call the landlord and ask for his guidance.

"Just wait until spring and see what comes up. Then you can tell what's dead and what's alive." I took his advice.

When spring arrived, everything came up! Daffodils, crocuses, hydrangeas, and azalea bushes blazed in full bloom. The crepe myrtle trees came fully alive. There were even several vegetable and herb gardens that bore fruit. I couldn't believe what I was seeing. The whole property looked like it had resurrected from the dead! The plants and schrubs I thought were dead and had been willing to cut down were now in full bloom. My colorful, burgeoning yard taught me a great truth: Life and death happen at the same time. The plants I thought were dead only looked that way because they were barren and brown and fruitless. However, put in their right season, those same withered plants burst into glorious life. Could it be that it was now my season to see my relationship with my mother, which had seemed barren and dead for so long, now come alive, simply because it was a new season?

The challenge was to keep my eyes on the vision of spring, even when all around me were signs of winter. I believe God was trying to show me that I had to hold onto the invisible to see the impossible become reality. I was challenged to see, not with my natural eye but my spiritual eye, and to believe in the promise of new life—*now!* Though Mom and I were caught in a great emotional struggle to live in that house in the midst of rapid change, fresh signs of spring in our relationship were well on the way.

Life Signs

Every house I lived in represented a different type of emotional reality. I mentioned previously that my childhood home was a place of emotional vacancy, and my Chesapeake home, a place of emotional violation. When Mom lived with me in Florida, that home was where I took emotional and spiritual authority. The old grey house in Virginia Beach would become a home of emotional connection, despite all our difficulties.

I don't know how to define the invisible but very real tug of war that goes on between a mother and daughter, or parent and adult child in general. I do know the purpose of parenting is to raise a child who can eventually "leave the home." But you can't leave someone emotionally if you have not first bonded to that parent. Separation has to follow connection. As an adult, I was still trying to connect with my mother and then somehow leave. Was I wasting my time? I know of other adults who have had the same kind of struggle, but they find it within themselves to just "leave." To them it isn't important to them to find a meaningful connection.

Was it the early death of my father at a critical time in my own upbringing that birthed the great desire, and even perhaps desperation, to secure a relationship with at least one of my parents? I think so.

My struggle was further compounded by Mom's age. At the

same time that I was trying to reach Mom's heart, I was experiencing role reversal. Because she was beginning to shut down, I was becoming her parent, and she was to some extent becoming my child. How could I preserve her dignity of soul as a mother and woman while simultaneously building a rich relationship with her?

Some days were better than others. Sometimes I felt a great deal of anger and took it out on her. I didn't know why. The best scenario would have been for us to have our own physical spaces in separate houses, but here we were. I somehow felt that God in His wisdom had created this time as a divine setup to work through those very issues. I didn't know that in coming to my mother I would also be coming to myself. There were things I would have to look at and discover in my own soul. She was a mirror to me, not only of myself, but also of learning to live life.

As an athlete, my sole way of relating to the world was one of performance. The life of the soul, however, is not about achieving. It's about being and becoming. Henri Nouwen's writings on what it means to be alive helped me to understand the difference between living life and accomplishing goals.

How do you know if you are alive? How do you produce life? As I read from *Life-signs* and his other writings, I came to understand that my aim was not to change my mother, but to reach her—not to have us "go somewhere" as much as to "be somewhere." The challenge was to create an environment of life.

Nouwen describes three life signs: care, vulnerability, and gratitude. When I care for somebody or allow somebody to care for me, it's saying, "I need you. I can't live this life on my own and through my own resources." It means giving to another love and provision, and it breeds life in another human being.

Vulnerability means I allow myself to show my weak side. I expose that part of me that needs another human being. We cannot receive love when all we show is our strong side. When I allow myself to be vulnerable, I invite someone else's strength to attach to my weakness, and I come alive.

Gratitude means that I acknowledge the value of what someone else has imparted to me. By my receiving their care and love, it gives that person worth and appreciation, and builds them up.

When we cultivate an atmosphere of care, vulnerability, and gratitude, we create life. I'm convinced that the main atmosphere of the home should exhibit these qualities.

In reading Nouwen, I began to understand the dynamics I would need to create in "our" new home environment if I wanted to experience true transformation.

Come spring, after we had navigated through the trials of moving and altered circumstances, the life signs began to blossom.

Backyard Golf
and the Peace Couch

*O*ne of the most beautiful things about our new home was the spacious fenced-in backyard. Set on a few acres of land, the yard for Teddy-boy was doggie heaven. All day long he ran around chasing squirrels and exploring the smells. His room was the screened-in back-porch where he could keep watch over the property.

On one side of the yard were three beautiful crepe myrtle trees. As I walked off the yard from one end to the other one day, I discovered we had plenty of room for a mini-driving range. Mom liked the idea of practicing in the backyard, too. I asked her if she would like to hit some golf balls.

"Sure," she said with curiosity.

"Here, try this sand wedge. This was Daddy's club. I think you'll like it. It has a lot of loft on it and you'll get it in the air easily." I teed up the ball while Mom carefully wrapped her fingers around the club.

She enjoyed being a student and learning a new skill, even in her late eighties. I noticed that while in golf she easily submitted to instruction, in other areas she refused to comply. If she felt she was an expert in certain kinds of work or in the kitchen, watch out. You better not tell her what to do! With golf being outside her area of expertise, she had no problem following instructions and had no battle to fight. "This is great!" I thought. "I'm connecting with Mom and she's letting me impart my gift to her." I loved releasing her athletic ability. This brought great joy to both of our hearts to be in the backyard together with Teddy racing around us.

"Hold your fingers tighter around the club," I directed. Mom proceeded in her usual fashion of taking a big backswing with a full shoulder turn. As she swung down with grace and strength, she hit the center of the ball. It went sailing sixty yards, all the way to the other end of the yard. "Mom, that was great! You're a really great golfer!"

She grinned, acknowledging her feat. "I know. Put another ball down." We both smiled with excitement.

For the next half hour, I watched Mom hit perfect shots into the crepe myrtle trees, with some sailing over the fence into the next yard. It was a moment to behold. She was proud of her developing skill.

We had many moments like that—Mom, Teddy-boy, and me, tooling around the back-yard, hitting balls, laughing, the dog joining us in playful banter. I'll never forget those times for as long as I live.

The fun we shared outdoors reminded me that despite the inadequacies of family life when I was growing up, there were good times, too. My brother and I enjoyed playing in our backyard. We hunted for lightning bugs, played in the tree house, and rocked back and forth on our patio lounge, enjoying the cool evening breezes.

Another place of "soul growth" for Mom and me was the back porch. One day, we were arguing, ready to pull one another's hair out. I'm sure it was over nothing, but we were having another one of our daily tiffs. Finally, I just said, "Mom, let's get out of here. Let's just go shopping." I had to think of something quick. We were both going crazy.

As we drove down the narrow lane on Cedar Point Drive, we noticed a nice-looking blue and white striped couch sitting on the side of the road. A neighbor had obviously put it out for the trash. Mom and I quickly smiled at one another, thinking we'd just won the lottery. "Are you thinking what I'm thinking?" I asked her.

"Yes! Stop the car and let's check it out!"

I pulled over and Mom sprang from the car and started inspecting the couch. "Well, it's a bit dirty. There are several tears in the material, and the pillows need to be filled up." After her assessment, she turned to me and proclaimed, "I can get it looking good in about a day's time!"

It was a high-end couch, actually a sofa bed. I needed a couch for the back porch, and this would be perfect! "Mom, let's take it!" I agreed with her assessment and was equally thrilled about finding our new treasure.

I noticed that the yard man was finishing up cutting the grass and asked if he would deliver the couch on his trailer. Within a few minutes we had a new couch on the back porch! Immediately, Mom and I sat down on it. "This is great!" she said. I couldn't believe the change of atmosphere between us.

I called the couch our "peace couch." It was a couch with a higher purpose, because when Mom and I sat there, we took our eyes off of one another and out onto the view. As we soaked in the lush, green landscape, we breathed in the peace, forgetting our petty disagreements.

I was catching onto the lesson I was supposed to be learning here. Change the atmosphere; don't seek to change the other person. Enjoy each other with a shared focus. The couch became an amazing "prop" on the stage of our relationship where we discovered the blessing of true companionship. Mom had our peace couch looking like new in just a day. In no time at all, she had washed off the dirty spots, filled up the anemic looking pillows, and sewed up the ripped places. That old trashed couch became our mutual treasure!

A few weeks later, I walked down the street to check out a yard sale our neighbor was having. It happened to be the same residence from which we had rescued our peace couch. I met the lady of the house and immediately shared our joy. "I hope you didn't mind our taking your trashed couch," I said. "I just had to tell you how much we are enjoying it. We live in the big grey house at the end of the street. That couch is perfectly situated on our back porch, and gives us great pleasure as we look out on the yard."

The woman looked at me with surprise and delight. "Well, you know, we used to live in that very same house. We bought the couch for that back porch." I couldn't believe what I was hearing. To think that in my first conversation with this neighbor, I learned that our peace couch was now on its second mission to bring joy and happiness to the dwellers at 1261 Cedar Point Drive. It was simply amazing and much too coincidental not to think that God, too, was having a little chuckle along with us.

More Life Signs

Coming to understand the lesson of nature that "life and death happen at the same time," I could see both Mom's development and decline—life and death—happening to her on a daily basis. It was my aim to keep focused on producing life in her and between us, while acknowledging her steady decline. I was often reminded of what the Apostle Paul said: "Though our outward man is [progressively] decaying and wasting away, yet our inner self is being [progressively] renewed day after day."

Emotionally, I saw how hard it was for her to relocate at her age. Her capacity for change and flexibility were waning. For the first two months or so, she cried almost every night, and I would end up crying with her. It was hard for her to be removed from familiar surroundings. Even though she didn't have any friends in North Carolina, she did have a son, whom she missed greatly. We were emotionally needy in our own ways and for different reasons. Seeing Mom's decline made me all the more want to find ways to bring new life to her.

We found that new life in many different and sometimes surprising ways. Sometimes it came in little ways and at other times in big leaps. One of the little ways we found a fresh emotional connection was in playing checkers.

Whenever Mom would get into a competitive situation, her brain really fired up. She beat me often and would win an entire series of games. "Mom, I can't believe you just killed me in checkers! And I'm trying my hardest."

"That's because I'm good!" she'd reply. She was so proud of herself when she won at checkers, and would get furious when she made a bad move. I don't understand how the brain works, but it was obvious some part of her brain was fully functioning when she got into a competitive mode.

She was also gifted at hospitality. Every now and then I would invite my friends over for a gathering at the house. Mom was so happy to fix food and welcome people into the home.

Perhaps the biggest leap we took to give Mom a new sense of life was in my helping her start her own housecleaning business. This came about because she would clean our house up to five times in one week, and it was driving me crazy. "Mom! If you like housecleaning so much, why don't we see if the neighbors would like your services? It would get you out of the house, and you could make some good money."

"Let me think about it," she said. "I don't want to be in a situation of having to work."

"You would only have to work when you wanted," I replied. "Considering your condition, I think you could work for a maximum of three hours. That's what you do here. What do you think?"

"Sounds good to me," she said. "But how will I get customers?"

"That easy. All I need to do is make up a flyer. We'll call your business 'Spic and Span Housecleaning with Master Professional Mildred Karaman. Housecleaning the Old Fashioned Way.'" Mom perked up at the idea. I could tell it made her feel important. "I'll make up twenty flyers and mail them to everyone on the block," I suggested. And that's just what we did.

In no time, we started getting calls. Mom made up to twenty-five dollars an hour, all cash. Her clients told her how pleased they were with her. It was evident that every time she came home, she felt fulfilled, having met new people who were grateful for her work.

One time she helped clean my friend's house. Later the friend called to tell me what her fifteen-year-old son said when he came home from school. "Mom, that was an old lady cleaning our house! She was cleaning like it was nobody's business! Once she started, she kept going. I've never seen somebody work that hard nonstop!"

That was Mom! She made housecleaning an Olympic sport. Another time I went with her on a job to clean the home of a single man named Rod. He left for about four hours. During that time, Mom spent an extra hour going to town—wiping the floors, vacuuming, dusting, and washing everything in sight. When Rod returned, she was dripping with sweat.

Here was my mother, an old white woman, looking up into the face of a single black man. Not only was she sweating profusely, she was crying. "Thank you so much for giving me the chance to clean your house," she said. I couldn't believe what I was seeing. Mom was in her glory, doing what she did best—making people's homes sparkle with cleanliness, and working like an athlete in the process. Rod looked down at her, and gave her a big hug. "Mama, you did a fine job!" Mom smiled, beaming from ear to ear.

On the way home I asked her, "Why were you crying in there?"

"I was so glad to clean his house because I knew he really appreciated it. It made me feel good."

I was so glad to see Mom in her glory. I was also sad, because she derived most, if not all, of her worth from her work. She really didn't know who she was apart from "doing."

It's easy to see the wrong in our parents and how they failed us. It was important for me to understand my mother and why she was the way she was. Detaching myself emotionally from her, standing far enough back to just observe her as a person was a valuable practice for me. Sometimes I didn't understand her, but watching her in action, as when she cleaned Rod's house, and seeing her response, helped me to grasp the way she viewed herself.

If we want to perceive the truth about something, we have to practice enough emotional detachment to be able to clearly see a thing for what it is, not for what we want to inject into the equation from our own perspective or need.

I spent a lot of time creating new atmospheres for Mom with what I call "shots of joy," experiences of emotional connection between us. In doing so, I had serendipitous opportunities to discover aspects of her that would reveal themselves in the most unsuspecting moments. Those moments became my treasures. They made all the warfare worth it. I believe that to know and be known is the highest gift we can give to one another.

I recall with joy the many new environments Mom and I shared. Our back porch and yard became an incubator space for renewal. I came to know Mom in places where she could enjoy activities according to her own speed and strength, not mine—things like hitting pitching wedge shots sixty yards in the backyard, playing with the dog, beating me at checkers, and launching her little housecleaning business, which empowered her.

But over time, care giving and its emotional demands took a toll on me. I didn't know much about being a caregiver at the time, but if I had to do it over again, I would have enlisted a host of friends to help out. You simply cannot do it all by yourself. It was at that point that I cried out to God for help. And He answered in the most surprising way.

Legacy Vacation

*M*y friend Shelley called me one day, inviting me to meet her best friend, Linda, from Washington, DC. I looked forward to meeting Linda because I'd heard of her outstanding work with college students in DC. She and her husband, a former senator, started a successful program for budding leaders. Because female leaders who share my same interests is a rare thing, I could hardly wait to talk with her about my own work with students and aspiring leaders.

When Sunday came and we sat down for breakfast on my porch, we immediately began sharing at a deep level. What I thought would be a conversation about common work interests never took place. Instead, Linda took the lead to ask me questions about my own life. Somewhere in the midst of our conversation, she began inquiring about my mother and the nature of our relationship. Sensing something was there that was unresolved, she asked, "What is the lie you're believing that is keeping you stuck from moving on with your life?"

"Hmmm," I said to myself. "I do this with other people! They don't do it to me." I suddenly realized that this was a divine appointment sent my way to help me uncover some truth about myself. Taking a moment to reflect, I opened up my heart. What surfaced was a deep and lifelong fear of going out into the world. "I was never nurtured emotionally growing up," I told Linda.

"Consequently, the world to me is not a safe place— not a place I can safely venture out into." As the words popped out of my mouth, I became surprised at my answer, never having given thought to my insecurity that way before.

"I'm going to pray for you about the root of your feeling unsafe in the world and ask God to heal it," Linda said. "God wants you healed, Veronica, and to move on with your life. Do you really want to live with your mother?"

After a good long thought, I replied, "No. I just want a good relationship with her for us to create lasting memories together." Linda and Shelley prayed for me, and as I wept, they asked God to bring wholeness to my fractured soul.

After they left, I began to think about getting my life on track and how I could create an unforgettable experience with my mother. About this time, I received an invitation to play in the Canadian Women's Open Qualifying Tournament in Nova Scotia, Canada. Although it caught my attention because I couldn't figure out how they got my address, I kept dismissing the opportunity. Canada was too far. I didn't have the money to go. Not only that, I hadn't played competitively for four years. At the same time, I couldn't throw it away. It was as if it had my name written all over it, but I just couldn't muster up the faith to act on it. What I did do was begin to pray, "Lord, if you want me to attend this tournament and also make it a vacation with Mom, please show me." Confirmation came, not just once, but several times over.

Later that week, I attended a ladies' Bible study at church. After sharing my request before God, Lu Wiley, who was in the group, said, "My brother, Red, lives in Nova Scotia. I would be delighted to call him for you. You could stay with him and his lovely wife." This was a significant confirmation because I knew I didn't have the funds to stay a whole week in Canada and pay for the rest of my expenses.

The following week brought another confirmation. I was doing a radio production and told my friend Jeff, the producer, that I was thinking about going to Nova Scotia. He lit up. "My wife and I went on our honeymoon there." He happened to have a map of the world in his office and showed me all the good tourist spots, including Peggy's Cove, Lunenburg, the Cabot Trail, and other spots. I carefully took notes on each one.

Once home, I announced to Mom my plans to play in the Canadian Women's Open Qualifying Tournament in Nova Scotia in mid-July, explaining there was a small chance that I could qualify. If I didn't, I would spend the week on vacation with her. I said, "I think we're supposed to go and create a lasting memory. Are you up for the adventure?"

"No, I don't think so," Mom replied, quickly dismissing my invitation. "I'm too old!"

I disagreed. "I really believe we are meant to go on this trip. So, first things first. We need to find out if you have a birth certificate. If not, I'll see about getting you a passport. If we can get you the documents you need to travel, I think we should go." Reluctantly, Mom agreed.

We had only a few weeks to get all our ducks in a row. I found out that Mom didn't have a birth certificate because it wasn't required back then. My next step was to see about getting her a passport. Because she didn't have a birth certificate, I had to make several calls to the diocese of Pittsburgh to see if they had a record of her birth. In one day, three people from three different cities had to coordinate and follow through with faxing and mailing to get all the necessary paperwork in on time. Miraculously, they all came through. I just had to keep moving forward, doing everything I could to do to make this trip possible.

Heading to the post office was our next step. By this time Mom's faith was beginning to rise. "If my passport comes through, I'll go," she said. She still had a frown on her face, but luckily we encountered a comical lady at the passport office.

"Now, Miss Mildred, if you're going to take a passport picture, you're going to have to smile. No grouches are allowed in here." It was just enough for Mom to crack a smile and realize this wasn't a heavy ordeal.

I whispered to the lady, "Please don't let my mother know it's going to cost a couple hundred dollars to expedite the process." The passport lady agreed and continued to chuckle.

"Now Miss Mildred, you see that nice gentleman behind you? I'd be happy to fix you up on a date with him."

The man's face turned red. "No thank you," he mumbled. By now, Mom was laughing and ready to head to Canada.

Not long after, the passport came in the mail. I couldn't wait to open it. "Mom, it's here!" We opened the envelope and slapped a high five. "We're going to Canada!" Seeing that faith works, Mom was on board with me.

I had to exhaust every possibility to obtain that passport, and with all the effort it took to get it, I was determined to get from our trip all that God had in store. My determination would come in handy. The fight to get to Canada had just begun.

In making our travel arrangements to Canada, I spent weeks trying to find the most expeditious route. After all, my mother was old, and I had to be careful about her heart condition. I was able to find a flight that had only one connection from Norfolk, a flight with Continental Airlines that went to Newark and then on to Nova Scotia. The flight time was only four hours, so I booked it.

I called and asked Lu if her brother and wife would be open to Mom coming with me. I didn't want to overstep their graciousness, but I knew housing was an issue. Lu discouraged me from taking my mother with her health condition, explaining to me how rugged the trip was and that she didn't think Mom would feel comfortable at the house. Red and his wife had a young baby, and she was concerned about all the dynamics. I called Red and he assured me that we both were welcome and it wouldn't be a problem.

Keeping Lu's concern in mind, I decided we would keep pressing forward with our plans.

Off to Canada

*A*fter arranging a myriad of other details, I welcomed the day that finally arrived, July 8th. Mom and I eagerly checked in our bags, only to find out shortly thereafter that the plane to Newark had been delayed indefinitely. "What's going on?" I asked the agent.

"Bad weather in Newark. You have the option of waiting or coming back tomorrow morning." The line was very long, and I didn't know what to do. Not wanting to make a decision without talking to Mom, I told her what happened. Seeing her anxiety, I persuaded her that we should just come back the following morning.

I got into another line and spoke with a different agent. He rescheduled us for the following morning and assured me everything was taken care of. "You don't need any other ticket. Just be sure to be here at 5 a.m."

We rose early the next day and arrived at the airport at 5 a.m., just like the agent told us to do. When we checked in at the counter, the agent gave us some surprising news.

"You're not in the computer. You're not even scheduled for this flight."

"What! We were here yesterday and were told everything was taken care of." After a huge battle with two agents and a supervisor, I showed them the writing on my ticket to prove my point. Finally the supervisor admitted, "Yes, that is Jack's writing. He made a mistake." They offered no apology but were finally able to get us on the flight.

Mom and I were shaken. Our vacation was already a day late, and now we were told we weren't in the computer. The supervisor assured me that it would be easy to get a connecting flight from Newark to Nova Scotia, so that was somewhat comforting—that is, until we landed and found out otherwise. Once we arrived in Newark, we went to the gate and were promptly told that we had missed the connecting flight and wouldn't have been able to get on it anyway. We were not in the computer.

I couldn't believe it. Fuming, I headed to customer care, where I promptly realized the title of the department was wrong. It should have been "Customer No-Care." The gentleman at the counter wrongly explained the problem to me, "The reason you're not in the computer is because you never showed up at the airport!"

"What do you mean, never showed up at the airport? We were there at 5 a.m. this morning!" To think this agent was telling me I was lying! I was furious. Then, pointing to a telephone, he said, "You have to go over there to call customer care if you want to reach a solution." I marched straight to the phone, and after a half hour of talking with another supervisor, was assured that she had booked us for the 6 p.m. flight, but that we were not scheduled for any return flight. By this time I was ready to blow up the entire airport. After another round of arguing my case, the agent assured me all our return flight arrangements were back to normal.

At no time during this fiasco did anyone offer an apology or to right the wrong. After hanging up the phone, I dragged myself over to my mother, exhausted from the emotional war I had been through. I could see the stress and uncertainty on her face.

I felt like a worn-out rag and started to cry. Mom reached for my hand and offered encouragement. We sat in silence as I cried. After about fifteen minutes, which seemed like an eternity, I felt better. Actually, it felt good to express my anger and get it all out instead of bottling it up as I usually did.

I announced our fate for the day to Mom. "We're going to have to spend the entire day in the Newark airport." Totally frustrated, I said to myself, "If we've had to go through all this garbage just to get to Canada, I am determined to get what we came for, even though I don't know what that is!" At any point along the way, we could have canceled our trip and just gone home. Although it was tempting, we didn't. But now stuck in the airport, I hadn't a clue as to what to do.

Then suddenly, despite my exhaustion, I felt a creative spark. It was time for a shot of joy. I pulled out my notebook and wrote on one page: "What I learned about you today." On the other side I wrote for my mom, "What I learned about you today." After scribbling how impressed I was with how Mom had handled herself, I thrust the book into her lap. "Now it's your turn." She took the notebook and began writing. When she was finished, I grabbed the notebook and put it in my carry-on.

I needed some kind of recovery. I could also tell Mom's heart was stressing from all the walking and emotional turmoil we had just been put through. We decided to simply go outside and sit in the sun for a few minutes. It was there I got another fresh spark.

A Well Deserved Break

*T*here we were, sitting on the grass outside the Newark airport, a day late going to Canada. I desperately needed to recover my energy and get a fresh breath for the rest of the day. I had an idea, so I asked the rental car agent where the closest golf course was. She directed me to the Weequahic Park Golf Course, which was only about ten minutes away. Catching a glimpse of adventure, I thanked her.

As we drove to downtown Newark, I thought about how well Mom was handling everything we had been through. She was an absolute trooper during the whole ordeal. I don't know another person her age who would have handled all the hurdles we jumped over as gracefully as she did. Although I could tell she was worried and absorbed all my stress watching me, she didn't complain. She just patiently waited for me to work everything out.

Turning into the golf course, I gave a big sigh of relief, knowing I could get in some good practice. Soon I realized this was at no ordinary golf course. For starters, there was no driving range, just a net to hit balls into. As I walked to the clubhouse, it was obvious every golfer was looking at me rather strangely, or at least to say, with noted interest. Surveying the panoramic view around me, I noticed something for the first time in all the years I've been playing golf: I was at an exclusively Afro-American membership golf course. Not only was I the only blond, I was the only white person there. What a scream—an old woman and her frazzled golf pro daughter showing up at the only Afro-American golf course that golf pro had ever heard of!

Because my golf clubs were somewhere in the Newark airport, or maybe even on their way to Nova Scotia by now, I didn't have any clubs to play with. Thinking I could rent some, I asked the pro if there were any available. "Sorry, but we don't have any rental clubs. You can borrow this old putter if you want to."

I proceeded with the charity case, "How about borrowing a few of those used golf balls?"

"No problem," he replied.

"Well, at least I can putt a little," I announced to Mom once back at the car.

"I'll stay here and catch a nap while you putt," Mom said. "A good plan," I thought, and headed for the putting green. It felt good to soak up the warm sun on my stressed-out body. I knew it would help me to putt on the slow greens for even half an hour. As I was beginning to enjoy myself on the putting green, forgetting the drama that had unfolded earlier in the day, I noticed a group of men sitting under a shade tree, drinking a beer and having a good time. One of the men strolled over to me and started a conversation.

"I've been watching you putt, young lady. That's not the stroke of an amateur, you know."

I chuckled. "Hi. I'm Veronica. I'm a golf pro on my way to Canada. We got stuck here for the day, and I'm dying to play some golf, but I don't have any clubs."

"I'm Donald, and I would be delighted to have you join me. I have a cart. Let me go over to my friend Moses and see if I can borrow his clubs."

Donald came back after a few minutes with two sets of clubs on his cart. "C'mon, Veronica, let's go play!" Yippee! I was headed out to the course. Mom gave me a thumbs up from the open window in the car. She was glad to take a well-needed nap while I ventured out on the course for a tough match with Donald!

We had a blast playing about six holes, driving up and down the rolling hills of downtown Newark. Although I didn't play that well, letting Donald beat me by a whopping seventy-five cents, Donald admitted it was the best golf he had played in years. Must have been the male-female competition thing, as I had a great time, too.

Once back at the car, I introduced Mom to Donald. We took a picture, and after thanking Moses for his clubs, she and I jumped in the car and headed back to the airport. We had a splendid adventure right in the midst of all our travel troubles. Armed with fresh recovery for our journey, we headed toward the gate once again.

Finally On Board

*M*om and I finally got on the plane to Nova Scotia on the 5:45 p.m. flight, exhausted from a day of tormented travel with no sympathy from anyone for our plight. As daunting as it was, I was soon to find out there was a life-changing purpose for our adversity.

As soon as we arrived in Nova Scotia, the atmosphere of our travels immediately changed for the better. The first person we met was the rental car agent. "Welcome to Canada!" The lady greeted us with surprising warmth, her genuine smile and attentive eyes reigniting the extinguished energy of our souls. I was glad to be on Canadian turf.

Mom and I hopped into a nice black SUV. After an hour's drive, we finally arrived at Red's house—a day and a half late—but we were there, and happy to go right to sleep. My one practice round was the next day and I wanted to be ready.

Red and Cynthia were wonderful people. We were touched by their hospitality, and the detail of their care. I could tell, however, that Cynthia was stressed trying to take care of her baby and sell their house. So Mom and I decided to move on and stay at the Holiday Inn the next few nights as I turned my attention to golf.

Glenn Arbour Golf Course was an eye feast. I hadn't realize how pristine Canada was. Carved out of a mountain, the course was exquisitely beautiful, with hills that went straight up and then straight down, many of them opening up into a broad expanse of water below. The fairways were lined by Christmas trees. They were so perfectly aligned to one another, it was as if they were saluting us as we walked by.

The word was, you had to be in really great shape, even as an LPGA player, to get around the course. Being out of shape, I worried that I would have trouble with endurance. So taken by the beauty around me and engaging the moment of being immersed again in the world of golf, I hardly noticed the rigor required of me to strut up and down the hills.

My caddy, John, turned out to be an excellent caddy and companion on the course. I hit the ball surprisingly well that day, and the combination of a pleasant conversation with John on an extraordinary golf course made just the right ingredients for a perfect day, despite the fact that it was raining.

Once back at the hotel, I noticed Mom was settling in comfortably, and I was glad to have the time to chill. I began to think about my chances for qualifying for the Canadian Open the next day. It was fortuitous for me that many of the golfers hadn't been able to make it to Nova Scotia. Flights were cancelled from all over due to inclement weather and runway repairs that prevented planes from landing easily. The numbers grew from eleven to twenty-four spots for qualifying. I wasn't nervous, although I was reminded of something I felt the Lord had spoken to my heart while I was preparing for the trip. It was the word "bittersweet" and it was in regard to July 11th. Was I going to qualify for the tournament, which would prevent me from going on vacation with Mom? Or, would I not qualify and then have a week's time to be with her? Either way was bittersweet. I would soon find out my fate.

A Different Kind of Treasure

*T*eeing off the next day in the Canadian Women's Open was a thrill for me. This tournament is an LPGA event, so I was in the environment of world class players. Although I have played in many professional events, to play in an LPGA event was a rare privilege for me. I would be in the company of the best women golfers in the world qualifying, and hopefully playing with them later in the week.

My trusty caddy John met me at the course early that morning. Mom was able to catch a few pictures of me before I teed off. The tournament officials were great in taking care of "Miss Mildred." Knowing she would be in good hands and that I was in good hands with my caddy, I proceeded to the first tee. My first drive down the fairway was a decent one. Whew! What I had hoped to duplicate afterward, however, didn't transpire. I gave my round the best I could, but under pressure my rusty swing just didn't hold up. It had been too long since I'd competed and was able to execute the shots. After a long and trying day, I posted an unimpressive eighty-four, missing the cut by about five shots.

I was disappointed, but in a strange way, wasn't let down by my performance. Knowing what God had impressed upon my heart prior to the trip, I accepted the bittersweet outcome. It was His higher will for me to spend the week with my mother. As I was meditating on the Scripture that morning, I came across a verse that spoke about making the Lord your gold and not clinging to the kind of gold the world has to offer. It helped me to let go of my disappointment over my professional pursuit and embrace the higher gold God had in store for us on our trip. It was extremely important that I had this perspective, because if I didn't, I wouldn't have been as free and able to let go to experience a different kind of treasure. So with a divine perspective in mind, I set my sights on vacationing with Mom.

The only problem was that even though I had taken notes from Jeff on sightseeing spots, I was so caught up in my golf arrangements, I hadn't really planned out the vacation part. Mom and I would just have to be spontaneous about our vacation plans, but she didn't care. And quite frankly, neither did I. We were on adventure out in the Canadian wilds—and despite our travel adversities, we were loving it.

We celebrated the commencement of our new direction with a

glass of wine that night at dinner. It was the first time I saw Mom loosen up a bit. I think half of glass of Canadian wine was more than she could handle. I had to hold onto her as we left the restaurant. She was ready to go dancing, giggling up a storm. We were both certainly ready for some fun, and it was on the way!

Restoring Lost Treasure

*T*he next morning we were fresh and raring to go. One of the first stops I wanted to make was Peggy's Cove. Peggy's Cove is a famous tourist destination at the tip of the Atlantic Ocean, located about forty-five minutes south of Halifax, where we were staying. It was a small fishing town that was made up of huge rock formations shaped by melting glaciers thousands of years ago.

On our way to Peggy's Cove, we first stopped in downtown Halifax and decided to visit the museum at the harbor front. On our tour, we discovered a special collection of articles from the sunken ship the *Titanic*. It was fascinating to see recovered articles from the famous ocean liner, giving credence to us in a new way that this thing really happened. People lost their lives, and we were looking at remains they left behind. We also learned during our tour that Halifax is the city that received the dead bodies from the ship and buried them there. It was interesting to find out that Halifax was a recovery place for lost treasures. I was reminded again of what the Lord had kept impressing upon me regarding our trip to Canada: He wanted to restore to us some kind of lost treasure. Of course I thought that meant my golf career, but I was beginning to think that what God really had in mind was the treasure of reclaiming the lost relationship I never had growing up with my mother. Could it be that God brought us to this spot in the world, known for its recovery operations, to perform a special recovery operation in a mother-daughter relationship? I pondered these things as we continued our tour through the historical boats, nautical items, and lunch on the pier.

In the early afternoon we headed for Peggy's Cove. Driving south I noticed just how uninhabited Nova Scotia is. Compared to the States, there were very few people. The country seems to be about fifteen to twenty years behind us in technological advances. But what they didn't have in modern devices, they more than made up for with spectacular scenery. As we drove down the winding road to our tourist spot, we enjoyed seeing pine trees, blue sky, grass as green as green can be, with water lacing the road all along the way.

We soon came to our destination and noticed that nature's exhibition had taken a different course. The land around us rose into huge rock formations. We kept driving the narrow-winding roads until we arrived at the lighthouse. I held Mom's arm, providing a steady step for her as we climbed up the rock formations to peer out over the tip of the Atlantic Ocean. It was breathtaking! It's one thing to overlook a river or lake, but it's entirely different to know you are as far out as it gets, looking out at the expanse of water that leads to the other side of the world. After taking some pictures, we jumped in the car and were on our way.

This is What I Call a Vacation

*N*ot knowing where we were going to spend the night, I stopped at the welcome center and made a few calls. They were all booked up, except for one rather unattractive place. I didn't have a clue where we were going to lay our heads that night. We kept driving. About ten miles north of Peggy's Cove, a truck in front of me made a sharp left. I noticed the sign at the entrance of the road, one unlike any I had seen for accommodations. The sign read "Oceanstone: A Cottage Resort." Not thinking twice, I decided to make the left turn right behind the truck and check out the place. You couldn't tell what it looked like because we had to drive down a long dirt road that snaked through many trees. After a while, the narrow road opened up into a beautiful and colorful collection of cottages.

"Let's check this out!" Mom suggested. I was impressed with her positive and inquisitive thinking. I was usually the one to suggest things.

As soon as we parked, a fluffy little dog ran over to our car to greet us. "Look how cute!" Mom said, beaming at the welcome. "He reminds me of Teddy-boy." At the green building in front of us, a man was sitting on a chair outside the building working on his computer. "Must be the manager," I thought. "Interesting that he would do his work outside. I would, too, if I worked here. It's so beautiful and quaint."

As we walked toward the building, accompanied by the resort dog, the man came over to greet us. "Hi! I'm Ron, and this is my dog, Ernie. Welcome to Oceanstone Resort. Can I help you ladies?" He opened the door for us and made us feel right at home. I hadn't planned on paying for a week's worth of hotel rooms for our trip, but I knew we were supposed to be on this vacation. Everywhere we had looked, the price was about the same. Mom sure seemed to like this place, so I decided to check in.

"We'll stay for two days."

After getting checked in, Ron helped us with our bags. We learned that he was the owner of the resort. We were impressed that the owner would give us such individual attention and service, something we weren't used to in the States. We certainly needed that care after all the hoops we had jumped through the last several days on our trip.

Ron took us to the green building, the one on the left in the cottage section. We stayed in room number two. Mom loved it because all the furniture was made of wood and everything looked like it was a hundred years old, but somehow made to look contemporary, too. I call it "contemporary old" furniture. The room was small, but welcoming. We sure were glad to find a place we could call home for a few days.

"Now this is what I call a vacation!" Mom exclaimed as we unpacked. I thought it was an interesting comment. Although I had been on vacation for several days, this was the first time she thought of it as *her* vacation. Maybe Mom didn't think the golf part was her vacation, too. Maybe it was just mine. It dawned on me that it was only when we checked into Oceanstone that our vacation was starting together. It made me happy to know Mom had finally engaged her spirit in the adventure. I think everything that had transpired was mere preparation for what was coming next.

Destiny Moment:
In the Diamonds

*W*anting to do something vacation-like even though it was five o'clock in the afternoon, I announced to Mom, "Let's go canoeing!" So my eighty-eight-year-old mother and I headed down to the shore. Ron helped us pull the canoe out in the water enough so we both could get in. "Mom, you want a paddle?"

"No, I just want to sit. I'm tired." I agreed to do the paddling. I could tell Mom was a little scared, but I was proud of her for getting in the boat and venturing out. Ron made us feel comfortable and safe. "I'll keep an eye on you as you paddle out. You will love it. I'll take a picture of you out on the water."

"Okay, Mom, we're off!" I pushed as hard as I could against the ocean floor, backing up the canoe, and then turning us around and paddling away from the shore.

"Ohhhh!" Mom let out a cry of anxious excitement.

"This is great, Mom! We're finally on adventure together!" About a half of mile out, we were dazzled by the island of rocks to our left, the lighthouse to our right, and the unending body of water in front of us. "Let's go over to the lighthouse first and then make our way back to the island of rocks."

"No, turn left here!" Mom commanded. "Now turn right!" I could tell she was very uncomfortable giving orders while not having her own paddle to control things. I cracked up laughing. "It must be hard for a control freak to be in a canoe without a paddle. Mom, I'm the only one with a paddle, and I get to steer us wherever I want to go," I retorted jokingly. We both laughed.

I saw a side of my mother that had been there all my life—the controller—but for the first time was able to make light of it. It was the one trait in her that caused a lot of friction between us, like a great divide I could never jump over. Over-control always keeps people in their own separate emotional boats, because there is no "we" in it. It's just "you vs. me" because nobody likes to be controlled. It brought a lot of heartache to my relationship with her over the years. She never let me in emotionally. I was a stranger to my own mother—but now we were in the same boat together, enjoying our ride out on the tip of the Atlantic Ocean.

After paddling for what seemed like hours (although it was only about thirty minutes), I stopped. Mom and I also quit our quibbling, and turned our sights outward to the breathtaking beauty surrounding us: the setting sun, the absolute calm water, the huge rocks hugging the shoreline, the black and white lighthouse in plain view. Everything was clear and pure. It was a crystal moment.

Mom and I looked at each other. For one moment in time, we were fully present to one another. All the flurry of stressful activity and the rush of the days before came to a halt. In fact, it vanished in the midst of the calmest moment of our lives.

In that miraculous moment, there was nothing to do. Just be. Mom didn't have to compete with my golf to get to my heart. I didn't have to compete with her workaholic ways to get to hers. With no barriers to cross, Mom and I connected spirit to spirit for the first time in our lives. Looking at each other and smiling, we treasured the moment. It was one I would hold in my heart forever. There on the tip of the Atlantic Ocean in a canoe, God reunited a mother and daughter. Emotionally, we gave birth to one another in an odd but beautiful way.

Rowing back in as the evening darkness began to descend, I couldn't help but thank God that I hadn't qualified for the tournament, as I had just recovered an incredible treasure—my mother's heart.

Close to shore, we saw Ron waiting to help us pull the canoe back on dry land. "Hey, I trust you two had a good time out there. By the way, I caught a picture of the both of you in the diamonds."

"What do you mean, in the diamonds?" I asked.

He explained, "You know, the place where two boats used to tell each other where they were located. When one boat wanted to communicate with another about its location, the captain would say, 'We are in the diamonds,' meaning 'we are on the part of the water where the sun is shining down and making the water glisten.' That's where I caught you and your mom out on the water. You were in the diamonds."

Ron's comment was profound. In the exact place Mom and I connected in spirit, we were also "in the diamonds" on the water. God was obviously letting us know we had found His special and rare place of deep relationship, mirrored in the connection of sun and water at just the right angle, making the water dance with shimmering lights. From then on, I labeled every moment that Mom and I deeply connected to be in the diamonds.

An in-the-diamonds moment is the place where two people can be comfortable with one together and not feel the pressure to be someone other than who they really are. It's where people "shimmer forth" their most authentic selves and are able to receive the spirit of another in all its fullness, too. It's the highest place of being, an intersection of souls. You come out of that exchange energized, enlightened, refreshed. Just as you see the shimmer on the water only from a particular angle, experiencing an in-the-diamonds moment is also experienced only from a certain angle. You don't work it up, only open yourself up to the fullness of life in the exchange. Perhaps it isn't even an interaction between two people, but three—a moment where God's presence is in the mix, too, because you definitely come out transformed. Yes, being in the diamonds definitely includes a taste of the eternal.

I made it my aim to seek a daily in-the-diamonds moment with Mom. Our canoe adventure helped me understand what that moment would mean experientially. I no longer needed the big transformation but rather the prize of an eternal moment with Mom. This was the true adventure. I was beginning to understand what God had meant when He revealed to me through prayer that this would be a trip of recovering lost treasure and going to a place neither Mom nor I needed a paddle for. All we needed was to allow God to take us to that rare place of being. But our in-the-diamonds encounter was not over. In fact, it was just beginning.

(Here we were. ^)

100

Meaningful Moments

The next morning Mom and I decided to get up early and head south again toward Peggy's Cove. We stopped at the memorial of the Swiss Air Flight 11. We ventured out on the rocks once again and stopped at the huge rock commemorating the lives lost in the air crash and the local people who rescued them.

I was reminded once more of the *Titanic* and how Halifax was pivotal in the rescue process. I thought of what God had impressed upon me regarding Mom several years before with the word "rescue." When I was wrestling with Him about what to do about Mom and what "love" meant, I kept thinking about His question, "What is your mother's point of need?"

I recalled my response: "She needs to be rescued," and God's charge to me: "Well then, rescue her!" It was significant that Mom and I were now standing on the exact spot known for its rescue missions. Here I was right in the middle of my "rescue mission" with her. I was beginning to see that it wasn't just Mom who was being rescued, but our relationship. Wouldn't it be just like God to lead us to an incredibly symbolic and historical place to validate that the journey we were on was orchestrated by Him?

In our culture we tend to be afraid of getting too involved with other people, especially the elderly, so we stay on the fringes of their lives. With all the pain and turmoil Mom and I had experienced in living together, our launching off in faith toward one another was remarkably rewarding. Something bigger than "just trying to reach each other" was going on here. It was deeply meaningful, even eternal.

I stopped for a moment to reflect on all that Mom and I had discovered about each other. If I hadn't rescued her, I never would have known that she was a great athlete and a real trooper in times of adversity. She was a humorist, communicator, hurt child, tender soul beneath the outer crust, and an adventurer.

Could it be that God in His infinite wisdom had led Mom and me all the way to the tip of the Atlantic Ocean, to a place known for its recovery operations, to speak a word of accomplishment to me? Could He be saying, "Well done, Veronica, rescue mission completed. You did it, and you did it well. Just look at your Mom. She is full of life. Thank you for paying the price to partner with Me to love your mother." Tears came to my eyes as I pictured the smile on my heavenly Father's face. He had to be pleased with both Mom and me.

After walking on the rocks for a while longer, Mom and I headed back to Oceanstone for lunch. While eating a sandwich, I reached for my journal. The last time we had written in it was at the airport. I remembered that I hadn't read what Mom wrote, so I opened the journal. "Wait a minute," she said. "I'm not done writing in it."

"Okay. I'll write in it, too," I offered.

Our room had a wide shelf in it under the front windows. Mom and I could comfortably sit next to each other, look out into the resort's pretty front yard, and write our thoughts using our makeshift writing desk. I pulled out a separate piece of paper. While Mom wrote her thoughts in the journal, I wrote mine in response to the question, "What I learned about you today . . ."

Curious as to what Mom had written about me in the airport, I opened up the journal to her words, "I learned what an absolute trooper you were today in handling all the problems at the airport. At each step along the way, you solved the problem and made sure we got to where we needed to go. I was so proud of you. It made me feel good that all I had to do was relax and let you take charge. You were so wonderful."

I was stunned. I never knew Mom felt that way about me. Her words deeply touched my heart. Somewhere in the midst of all the travel troubles we had encountered, Mom saw me in a different light. Perhaps all that happened just to open up her eyes to see me as a responsible person in a new way.

Putting down the journal, Mom turned to me and said, "Here is the rest of what I wrote." Her words continued to penetrate my heart. "You were so wonderful the entire trip, planning all the details and taking care of everything along the way. I am having a great time. I now realize that you are no longer my little girl, but my wonderful daughter."

Not only was I now stunned, but speechless. My mother had given me her blessing to be my own person. Her words freed me, released me, healed me, all in one moment. "Mom," I inquired, "What made you say those beautiful things?"

"I don't know," she said. "It just came to me as I was sitting here."

We were caught up in another in-the-diamonds moment. I could feel hot oil flowing down all the fractured places of my soul, bringing healing to a lifetime of emotional hurt. No counseling, positive confession, achievement, or self-confident look could touch what those few words of spoken blessing by a parent did for me. Something inside of me was released to go on. Something inside of Mom was released, too. We hugged and for the second time, exchanged the treasure of presence and being.

I was grateful for the difficulties we had had with travel because without them, I never would have thought up the creative idea of sharing journal thoughts. Determined to get what I came for, I just got it—all of it. The effort, stamina, and courage it took leading up to that priceless moment was beyond anything I could have imagined, but through it all, we recovered the treasure that afternoon of a lost mother-daughter connection of spirit.

Why it had to come through writing first, I don't know. I discovered something about my mother, however. She really could express her heart, but it was easier for her to do it through the written page. As a writer myself, I came to perceive another dimension of Mom I'd never known before: besides being an athlete, she was also a writer.

The next few days we visited Lunenburg, one of the oldest cities in Nova Scotia, drove up to Cape Breton Island, went sailing, and then returned to Oceanstone for a few more canoe rides.

Ron was glad to see us. When we pulled up, we saw him sitting in his usual outdoor office chair, this time with his pet bird perched on his head. Reaching into a paper cup, he fed the bird Cheerios and said, "He expects me to feed him all the time." It was a hoot! I thought to myself, "How many other resort critters are there?" Ernie, Ron's dog, then ran over to Mom, who scooped him up in her arms. Giving him a big hug, Mom said, "We're glad to be back!"

We wanted our last day to be filled with the peace of mind and spirit we had come to love about Oceanstone. As we chilled out, there was at least one more treasure I had to uncover before we left. It would be revealed to me through a rare conversation with Ron.

Final Treasure:
Competition vs. Contemplation

*W*hen Mom and I drove into Oceanstone, we knew we had come to a special place. Just being in the atmosphere made us feel like we were home, although we were the farthest place away from home we had ever been. Perhaps it was the coziness of the small cottages. Perhaps it was the combination of beautiful flowers, rock formations, and the individual attention the staff extended to us. But when I think about it, it was the owner, Ron, who made us feel so special.

Ron was a television producer who had given up his career to pursue the resort business passed down to him from his family. If I recall correctly, he was one of four brothers who took the property, renovated it, and made it a memorable place for people to visit. His heart was for Oceanstone to be a place where broken relationships were restored. When he told me that after I had shared with him all that was going on with Mom and me, I marveled again at God's amazing plan. He brought us to a place dedicated to reconnecting hearts.

I wanted to talk to Ron because I knew he was a deep person, someone who had given up the rat race to serve people who needed to be restored from that grind. "People come in here all expired from life," Ron explained. "I see it in their eyes. When I talk to them, they can't even look at me. They just keep looking down. My heart is to see this place pump life back into them. And I see that all the time, too. After several days basking in the beauty of God's creation here, they begin to breathe deeply again."

Before I left the resort, I wanted to engage Ron in one more extraordinary conversation. I sensed there was a treasure he was supposed to deposit in my life, and I didn't want to leave without it. Again, after all Mom and I had gone through to get to Canada, I wanted every treasure that was mine.

In our last afternoon there, I asked if I could spend some time with him. "There's something I want to talk to you about." Without hesitation, he agreed. It wasn't as if he didn't have anything else to do. The responsibilities of daily upkeep of all the rooms, handling the business items, and then tending to the guests was enough to keep him going all day long. However, when it came to connecting to people, he was always available.

We sat out on the porch behind the main office, which overlooks the ocean. Gazing at the spectacular view, I got right to the point with my question. "Ron, this has been an incredible week for me. The first involved was intense competition. I had to focus all my thoughts on getting the ball in the hole. I fought the weather, grueling hills, and competed with the best women golfers in the world. And then the rest of the week was spent in an opposite world—not of competition, but contemplation. Two worlds at opposite ends of the spectrum. Knowing that you lived in 'the world' for a long time and now you live out in the middle of nowhere, I thought you could relate to my extreme experiences. How do the two mix? Is it one or the other?"

Ron was quick to respond. "It's not one or the other. It's both. You have to go out in the world and do your competing—which represents the work world for most of us. Then you retreat, and go inward to the still, quiet place. Nature helps most of us get to that place again. It's finding the rhythm and balance of going from one to the other that is the challenge. And you need both."

"Hmm . . ." I pondered. "Well, that's helpful because I've been wondering how to proceed with my life. There are these two opposite forces working within me, and at times I just don't know which path to pursue."

He continued to enlighten me. "There are so many spiritually hungry people in the world. I see them all the time when they come here. They don't even know what they're looking for. I would think that if you could talk about golf—the competitive side of life—what they understand—and use that as a means of explaining spiritual truths, you would be doing a great service to mankind. People need what you have."

His words spoke to the core of my being. His words were the treasure I needed to discover—an embrace of both sides of me— the inner, quiet world in conjunction with the outward world of action and exploration. Actually, both are worlds of adventure, focus, and action. They just require different types of energy. I wanted to know more, but I also wanted to turn my attention to him.

"Tell me about you, Ron. You were a television producer—do you still plan on pursing that someday?"

"I do," he said, "but I don't know how to fit that vision into what is already all-consuming for me here."

I contemplated what he said and asked, "Could you begin with a small step? It seems there should be a way to work your passion for television and producing into your passion here for helping people to grow more deeply." After we pondered and explored the possibilities, I suggested, "Have you ever considered videotaping some of your conferences here, or at least the stories of people who come here and are changed, and then put them on your website? It's a small but powerful way of combining your background as producer and at the same time growing your inner passion of helping to restore people's souls."

Just as I had lit up with Ron's insights, I saw a spark light up in him. "You know," he said, "not very many people understand my heart and vision. Thank you for taking the time to listen to me and then respond. There are people who listen but then aren't able to make any kind of contribution to my path. Thank you so much." It was one of those rare conversations, where you're given permission to enter into the soul of another person and walk down the conversational fairway with them. I walked it with Ron and it was wonderful.

I asked him if I could pray for him. Even though we didn't hold the same theology, we both were spiritual people, and I felt there was something I wanted to pray for him that was from the Father's heart. "Dear Lord Jesus, I pray for Ron. I pray that you would activate his dream, his vision, and cause everything You created him to be to come to pass. I pray that You would fulfill the vision of Oceanstone according to Your heart. Take this place that You created and cause it to usher forth new life into people's souls, and to usher forth new life into Ron's soul. Bless him and this place for being the agent of a transformed relationship between Mom and me. We will forever remember Oceanstone as the spot where You brought us both "in the diamonds"—spirit to spirit—for the first time in our lives. Amen."

After the prayer, Ron looked up at me. I could tell he was as moved by the divine moment of being the recipient of the prayer as I was by being the giver of it. I wasn't used to expressing the spiritual side of me in such a setting with someone I hardly knew, but in this case, I did "know" him—and wasn't afraid to let the God-part of me—the contemplator— express itself.

The conversation with Ron was one of the highlights of my trip. So many times we go sight-seeing on the outside and take in all that an area has to offer but fail to sight-see on the inside and get to know the people who cross our paths. Perhaps I should call it "insight-seeing." This was a trip that was both an outward and an inward journey.

After my talk with Ron, Mom and I packed our bags. The plan was to drive back to Halifax and spend the night at the Holiday Inn. Our flight was scheduled for eight o'clock the next morning, and we wanted to shorten our drive time as much as possible.

After checking into the hotel, we decided to go to a spare ribs place for dinner. Seated next to us were two officials from the Canadian Women's Open. I had almost forgotten about the tournament, even though I managed to back there one day to watch the action. Excited about our week's adventure, I said to the ladies, "I came up to qualify for the tournament but didn't make it. I did get to spend a week's vacation with my elderly mother, however, and we had a wonderful time. This may be the last vacation together because she has a heart condition, and we're both glad to have made the trip." One of the officials remarked, "The tournament was great, but it sounds like the most important thing was spending time with your mom." Mom and I looked at each other and smiled, because we both knew it really was the most important thing!

While waiting for our food, I took the crayons on the table and began to draw everything I could remember about our week: a sailboat, a canoe, golf clubs, and two stick-figure women smiling with their arms around one another. Over all the drawings I wrote, "It was the most important thing."

I was glad we came to Canada. It was an unforgettable week, not to mention the surprise that was still awaiting me at the airlines. Wanting to be sure the same fate we had encountered on our outbound flight wouldn't recur on our homebound one, I decided to call the airlines once we arrived back at the hotel. After a marvelous day, the last thing I wanted was another fiasco with the airlines. Unfortunately, the drama continued as I discovered we were deleted from the computer again. I couldn't believe it.

Was I going to lose my cool again, or could I retain it? The last thing I wanted to do was to lose my peace, but here we were going home, and I had no certainty we could get on a plane, despite the fact that we had made our flight plans weeks ahead of time. After being on the phone with a supervisor for over an hour, she assured me we were rebooked for our original flight. I had talked with at least six people, and this lady was the first to offer any real customer service. She apologized for the trauma the airlines had caused us, especially my mother. I had to wonder how any airlines could stay in existence with the total incompetence and lack of customer care we'd been subjected to from start to finish on our trip.

The good news is, we made it home okay. Around nine-thirty that evening, after we had unpacked, the phone rang. It was a call from the airlines, stating, "We're sorry we had to make alternate plans for you. There has been a delay in your flight. Please call us to make other arrangements." "They have got to be joking," I thought. "We're already home from our trip and the airline is still harassing us! Ahhh!"

It didn't matter, however. I learned to love my mother, and I finally had a lasting legacy of memories from our trip.

Receiving My Trophy

Going to Canada was certainly a watershed experience. I don't know why Mom and I encountered all the adversity we did, but in retrospect, I've been able to draw some valuable insights. Sometimes in our attempt to connect with another person, we think we have to change them before we can have a relationship. Discovering the "in-the-diamonds" concept, I realized that I didn't have to spend my energy trying to fix Mom anymore. Of course, I was too blinded with pride to admit that I probably needed more changing than she did. The Canada trip gave me a new strategy—it wasn't about changing at all but about reaching, finding the right angle in a given situation, creating an atmosphere, or even changing the atmosphere to experience what we did on that water with our in-the-diamonds connection. Setting up a shot of joy was the process I would apply to my in-the-diamonds relational target. It was a brilliant concept that would become a transformational strategy for me in times to come.

The strategy that would further propel Mom's and my new trajectory of relationship was a willingness to have my values changed. It was easy for me to value the temporal trophy of a tournament bid. It was much harder for me to value small, seemingly insignificant moments with my loved one. After all, I was trained to be an achiever. To find the treasure, I had to be open to redefining what the true treasure was. Because I allowed

113

that redefinition to occur, I was most surprised when I was rewarded with a real trophy.

Shortly after arriving home from Canada, I received a phone call from my friend, Pam. "Veronica, I have a gift for you. I discovered this about six months ago and immediately thought of you. I just haven't had the time to give it to you. Can I drop it off this afternoon?"

When I opened the gift, I was stunned. It was a golf trophy. Unlike the typical bowl-shaped silver trophy with handles on the sides, this trophy was different. It was in the shape of a woman, a classy woman dressed to the hilt. She was leaning on a golf club with one hand and had the other hand on her hip. I immediately grasped the trophy's symbolism of the trophy, as I explained it to my friend.

"Pam, I can't believe this. It was meant for you to hold that trophy until the precise moment it would be meaningful to me beyond what you could ever know. I just returned from Canada where I heard a Voice say to me that my trip would be 'bittersweet.' I wanted the trip to be about golf, but it was about a purpose higher than that. It was about forming a lasting legacy with

my mother. Because I listened from within and entered into that higher purpose, I believe God is giving me this trophy. It represents not achievement, but personal formation. The trophy is the figure of a person. I've achieved a higher level of personhood, and God wanted to award me with this trophy! Thank you so much!"

Both Pam and I were amazed at the love of God. He wanted to relate to me on my level through the trophy. I took it as a job well done—and rewarded by Him!

Shots of Joy

*A*fter Canada, I was excited to put my new in-the-diamonds strategy to work. While the first in-the-diamonds moment was spontaneous, I wanted to see how it would work to intentionally create such a moment. I had to pick on something that Mom and I could both equally share in and enjoy, and then create enough space in it for life to take place.

September was on its way, which meant we would be

celebrating Mom's birthday. I decided to put on the first Grandma Open, a golf event that would bring together the generations. Mom would be the honored guest. Friends suggested making it big and even getting the media involved. As things turned out, however, my efforts to create a grand event fell through. At the last moment, I invited fifteen of my friends, most of whom had never played golf, to join us for a few hours of fun at the First Tee Golf Course in Virginia Beach.

The First Tee is an outstanding junior golf program. What was special about the program in Virginia Beach was that it also had its own private golf course. Junior golfers could enjoy their own little clubhouse, practice range, and nine-hole golf course. Dick Wren, the director of instruction, helped out by giving a clinic to my friends.

We had an absolute blast! After the instruction clinic, we had a driving, putting and chipping contest. The participants' ages ranged from eight to forty-eight to Mom at eighty-eight. Inside the clubhouse we put on birthday hats and celebrated with cake. It was meant to be a small but meaningful time. My brother, Mike, came up from North Carolina. Mom was thrilled for us to be together.

The most precious moment came when it was all over. Mom came over to me, gave me a big hug, and said, "I had a really great time!" She was beaming from ear to ear. I'll never forget that moment. We expanded our in-the-diamonds experience to a group of people and birthed about ten new golfers that day! The shot of joy strategy worked!

I found the strategy to work especially well when I needed to change the atmosphere. One day not long after Mom's birthday celebration, we were in the heat of a big argument. The negative atmosphere was reaching a head. I knew I needed to do something quick, so I said, "Mom, let's get dressed up and go out for dinner." She looked at me like I was nuts. "Yes, I think that's what we need to do to change the energy here. Go put something nice on and I'll treat you." That's all she needed to hear.

Once at the restaurant, we had to wait because it was quite

busy, so we went to the bar area. "What kind of beer do you have?" Mom asked the waiter.

"We have Budweiser, Coors, and Pilsner," he said and mentioned a few other brands.

"Give me one of those Pillsbury beers," Mom ordered. She said it loud enough for the people next to us to hear. We all burst out laughing.

"Mom," I tried to explain, "Pillsbury is the dough you cook with. The beer is called Pilsner!"

She chuckled. "Oh, what the hell. It's all the same to me!" That was our shot of joy for the evening. From then on we had a good meal and a great time, as we turned the negative energy into positive energy at will.

Another shot of joy occurred when we were out on the golf course. This was the first time Mom had played in a foursome. I was always careful to consider how to integrate her into the normal flow of things, but always according to her ability. This particular day we were teamed up with three men. They always played together, but gladly allowed Mom and me to join them. They got such a kick out of watching Mom hit the ball. To keep the pace of play going, Mom would start her hole about a hundred yards out. It was the first time she felt she was part of a group out on the course. The day was pleasant and sunny, a perfect day for golf. I was proud of her for not being self-conscious with the men. She kept her confidence and fit right in.

After our nine-hole round, we walked back to my car. Mom stopped for a minute and paused in a rare moment of self-awareness. "What is it?" I asked, wondering if she was okay.

Pausing again, as if becoming aware of something for the first time, she said, "I feel like myself."

I almost fell over. "What was that worth?" I asked myself. I had given up my life to help my mother ward off a death wish, and now here she was declaring the opposite spirit. It was a totally spontaneous self-discovery.

"Yes, just being outside, moving my body, and having fun. I feel like myself."

I had to wonder just how long it had been since she'd had that feeling, maybe decades. All I had done was put Mom in an atmosphere where she was performing, being with people, and having to demonstrate a skill, all at the same time. She loved the outdoors, so being in a natural environment added to her convergence of being. Mom had a shot of joy with herself. I was so glad she felt free enough to share her discovery with me. It was profound.

As I continued to apply my new-found "shots of joy" strategy, I began to further define what a shot of joy is. A shot of joy is an intentional invitation to another person. Its aim is to connect with that person spirit to spirit. It requires a careful observation of the other person. The shot of joy is a specific activity based on what the other person would enjoy doing—but also something you enjoy. You have to ask yourself, "What do I want?" Then you decide how you can get what you want based on what you think the other person will specifically respond to. Normally the choice is over a shared interest or mutually enjoyable activity that you both connect over. When you implement your shot of joy, it can't be done with concern for the outcome. All you can do is make the invitation.

Shots of joy are very powerful, because they introduce something new into something that is familiar. And, as I was learning, if you want to experience something new with someone, you have to DO something new.

One afternoon I was thinking about making a new connection with my mother. I asked myself, "What can I do that will introduce her to something new?" It's so easy to think that just because a person is old, she can't learn new things. It's doing new things that keep a person young. After some thought, I came up with a great idea and presented it to Mom.

"You know how I love public speaking, and I'm beginning to

get more and more opportunities to speak," I said. "This Sunday I've been asked to do the Sunday morning service at a church in town. I was wondering if you would like to introduce me?"

I knew I was taking a huge risk. Mom liked to pull surprises on me, and this was one situation that would be somewhat out of my control. It was worth the risk of being embarrassed, however. Without hesitation, Mom replied with a resounding, "Yes!"

"Okay, then, let's sit down and write out the introduction together," I suggested. After spending about an hour on the introduction, I left for the afternoon.

A few hours later, I returned, only to find Mom sitting in her rocking chair with introduction in hand. "I think I have it!" she exclaimed.

"Mom, were you sitting here all afternoon memorizing that thing?"

"Yes! Just listen to this . . ." She recited the introduction flawlessly until she came to my career highlight. ". . . and Veronica's career highlight was playing in the 1889 US Open!"

"Mom," I laughed, "I didn't play in the 1889 Women's US Open. I played in the 1989 one!"

"Oh, you have to add a little humor in there somewhere to get them loosened up!" We both cracked up laughing. Here was my mother, who had never spoken publicly in her life, telling me, the trained professional, how to connect with an audience.

I've often wondered where I received my gift of communication. I never would have suspected in a million years I got it from Mom. Sunday arrived, and I was scared Mom would suddenly become a loose cannon. "It's very important to me that you give that introduction just like we planned," I told her. "I don't want to be embarrassed, and I don't want any surprises."

"Well . . ." she hesitated. "I wanted to share something about Michael and how he graduated from West Point."

"That's great that you want to talk about your son, but this is not the time or place. You are introducing me, remember?"

"Well, okay," Mom complied.

There were a few hundred people in the service that day. The

119

pastor announced, "And now someone very special is going to introduce our guest speaker. Her name is Mildred Karaman." When the pastor called Mom up, she walked right to the podium, grabbed the microphone, and looked absolutely stunning in her black and white chiffon blouse. She rattled off the introduction flawlessly. ". . . and Veronica's career highlight was playing in the 1889 US Open...." The people laughed and clapped. Mom introduced me like a seasoned communicator. I was so proud of her!

Afterward, the people came up to her and loved on her. It was a new experience for Mom to receive affirmation from others apart from her housework. She loved every minute of it. So did I.

From then on, I made it a point to invite Mom to introduce me at every local speaking engagement. She loved it, and grew in her ability to communicate, inspiring hundreds of women. From a cloistered life-style, Mom became a public person. Her ministry was inspiring people. She spoke to young and old alike, whether it was to women at a business network meeting, social club luncheon, or high school tennis team. The teenagers especially got such a big kick out of her!

Mom even had her own professional modeling photo shoot. Encouraged by a writing professor, I contacted an editor at *Guideposts* to publish Mom's story. They did! Although I didn't like the way they changed the story to focus too much on the struggle, we loved the trip to Florida they provided. The photographer for the article thought Mom was a real natural. We loved posing in a myriad of golf poses together. It was a thrill for Mom to experience her first professional modeling shoot at the tender age of eighty-eight. She was becoming even more of a public figure, this time inspiring a reading audience of two million people!

I was delighted to see Mom blossoming in her gifts and talents at a season in her life when most people would just be shutting down. Joining me in these adventures spoke a lot of her love for me. I had to capture all I could while I could, because the day came that proved to be my first real scare.

The First Bad Scare

*W*hen you're creating shots of joy, it's always easier to remember the positive highlights. The stresses in Mom's and my lives were equally present. Not a day went by without some kind of challenge to overcome.

As I've described previously, living in the old grey house was a blessing that gave us beauty and stability. We both felt immediately at home there. The spirit of the home resided there from the families that had lived there for years before us.

However, we didn't expect all the problems with the heat and water, and never knew if either was going to work properly from day to day. Because the owners planned eventually to tear down the house, they weren't too keen on putting in new equipment.

On top of that, we had to sort through Mom's furniture and begin to sell off what she no longer needed. I think we had about three yard sales. I know we gave away some valuable antiques, but neither of us had the capacity of mind or patience to research the best way to get the worth out of her few valuable possessions.

It was then I began to experience the reality of this last season in her life. I know it was hard for her to let go of furniture that had been hers for a good part of her life. Although she was a trooper through all of it, after the yard sales, she wondered if she should have relinquished as much as she did.

As I mentioned before, I wish someone would write a

handbook on how to "do death well." We had to wade our way through so many issues with so little guidance. Perhaps we just didn't know how to consult someone.

One weekend when I felt it would be good for Mom and me to have some space apart, my friend Wanda called. "Veronica, we're going away for the weekend. Would your Mom be interested in house-sitting for us?" I thought it might provide Mom with a good opportunity to rest. She agreed. I gave her the phone number to the house, and after going over all the details, dropped her off at Wanda's, who lived about ten minutes away.

When I picked Mom up later that weekend, I was alarmed to hear what had happened. "I couldn't find your phone number. When I went to go to bed at night, I couldn't breathe. I was so afraid I was going to die." I knew there had to be a reason for Mom to be in that much of weakened condition. I felt horrible that she was unable to contact me. After much questioning, I discovered that she had gone into her "turbo cleaning mode," scrubbing Wanda's floors on her hands and knees, cleaning out her refrigerator, and doing numerous other chores she was not supposed to do. Instead of resting, Mom went to work. I never understood her obsession with cleaning, but it was an addiction to her as much as alcohol or drugs are to others.

A day went by and Mom had more trouble breathing. When she could hardly talk, I decided to admit her to the hospital. As it turned out, Mom had congestive heart failure, which fortunately was treatable to some extent. The doctors drained the water out of her lungs, but it would stay out only as long as she kept to a low sodium diet and didn't over-tax herself. Although her main problem was a bad aortic valve, when her heart couldn't pump the blood properly, fluid backed up into her lungs.

It was a real scare for me. As much new life as we were enjoying, I knew death was lurking around the corner. This was the first ghost to come knocking at our door. I didn't know how much longer I had with her. I lived with the fear that any day I could lose my precious mother. I also lived with an overcoming hope that God would alert me in advance when it was her time to go.

When the doctors first diagnosed her, they gave her six months to live. She had already outlived their prediction by three years. Mom was a fierce fighter, and I believe her self-denial was so strong that she really didn't believe she was as sick as she was diagnosed to be. She refused to believe she was going down.

In fact, after seeing her condition in the hospital, I wasn't sure how much she would be rehabilitated. But just one month after her congestive heart failure, she made an amazing comeback.

I Never Saw a Whale Before!

I was just as intentional about helping Mom take daily steps of recovery as I was about creating shots of joy. I helped her set mini-goals for walking. She quickly surpassed all the goals I set for her. Within a month's time, she walked almost a mile on the Virginia Beach boardwalk.

We were both surprised at her comeback. During one of our walks, as we approached the end of the boardwalk, I spotted an unusual sight a few hundred yards away on the shore. A dead whale had washed ashore, and a crew of people were there cutting it up into pieces. "Let's go check it out!" Mom exclaimed. It took a few minutes of very slow walking in the sand to reach the whale.

We stood back, watching the group of men cutting the huge, gleaming body into little pieces with knives. As Mom studied the operation, I could tell she was in deep thought. All of a sudden, she walked over to the supervisor and said, "Excuse me, miss, but don't you think it would be easier to cut up that whale with an electric chain saw?"

"M'am," the woman responded, "electricity and water don't mix well!" I thought it was so cute that Mom's mind was still working and figuring out better ways to do things!

As we walked back to the boardwalk, Mom's eyes widened as she exclaimed, "I've never seen a whale before!" She was so excited to make a new discovery! As much as it meant for Mom to experience something new, I was needing that same sense of freshness.

I wondered if I could create a shot of joy with my family for Christmas. Sensing this could be our last Christmas with Mom, I wanted to break out of the "same old, same old" routine of my traveling to my brother's for the holiday. I wondered what would happen if I shifted the atmosphere and invited them to come visit me to experience something new. Considering they had never traveled over the holidays to visit me, it was a risk to invite them to come. However, I set my resolve to experience something new, and decided to follow-through with my invitation.

My next thought was, "What kind of invitation would work for them? What would they possibly respond to?" I knew if I invited them for Christmas Day, that wouldn't work, so I thought about inviting them up for the weekend.

The other part of creating a successful shot of joy was making a commitment not to be attached to the outcome. This was big because you always risked getting a "no." I had to be open to that.

All shots of joy must begin with asking oneself, "What do I want?" For me, I wanted a new connection with my family, even if it was for only a day. With much courage, I emailed my brother my intention: "I love you and I would like to see you and the family for Christmas. However, I won't be coming down for Christmas. Instead, I'd like to invite you and the family to come here for a visit. We would love to see all of you."

It was short, truthful, and respectful. I shared what I wanted, stated my plan, and expressed myself from a place of relationship. I detached myself from having to control the outcome. I made a decision to accept whatever response I would get.

To my total astonishment, the entire family came for a visit! When they first walked in the door—Mike, Nancy, and their two college-age children, Rachel and Elise—there was a good bit of awkwardness. Being together was a new atmosphere for all of us. Teddy-boy came to the rescue. He did something funny that broke the ice. After opening up presents, we sat down for a delicious home-cooked meal. Mom was in her element cooking up a storm for both lunch and dinner.

That afternoon I took my family on a tour of all the great gift shops in Virginia Beach. Since my sister-in-law enjoyed pink flamingos, we went on a pink flamingo shopping spree. I think she picked up about twenty-five new ones of all kinds and was really blessed that the shopping spree revolved around her interests, although it was mainly about our being together as a family.

At dinner, we laughed, conversed, and all enjoyed one another's company. I even had a chance to share with them some of my coaching work as we all took a motivational gifts test later that night.

The most amazing part of all was that I had one perfect day with my family. Not one negative thing transpired that day. Not one. I will remember that day for the rest of my life—and every detail of it. Did anybody change? No. Just the atmosphere. Just as Mom never had never seen a whale before, and it delighted her soul to see it. I too, found delight in my perfect day with my family.

Tearing Down the House

I often wondered why Mom and I were led to our beautiful old grey house in the most exclusive part of Virginia Beach, Bay Colony, to live. The house gave us such joy and settlement, as most old houses do. Outside, we had relished the herb gardens, the glorious flowers, and huge back yard. Inside, we felt at home with the arched doorways, hardwood floors, and all the historical fixtures of a memorable family home.

But there were internal problems that caused us considerable worry. The renters before us took out the hot water heater, and from one day to the next, we never knew if we would have hot water. There were also problems with the heat. Steam heat is great but also very expensive. My winter bill was never less than $300 a month, and that was with the temperature kept at about 64 degrees. As much as we complained, the owners were unwilling to address the root problem—that of the home's internal workings—and had no intention of financing major renovations.

The neighbors were against tearing down the house, with its stately beauty and stature as the ideal family home. But the owners, who were builders, figured it wasn't it worth it to keep the house.

Before we knew it, Chris, the owner, called me one day. "Veronica, I have some good news and bad news for you. The bad news is, we've decided to tear the house down. The good news is, if you're willing to move out before your lease ends, we will put you up in one of our beach condos for free and also pay the utilities."

The last thing I wanted to do was move again! Financially, it would help me out, but emotionally I knew it would be a disaster. Regretfully, we did decide to move, and I think the stress on both Mom and me took its toll.

One day after moving to the beach condo, I went back to the house to gather a few more things out of the garage. To my shock and amazement, when I drove up to the house, I saw a huge bulldozer right in the middle of the house, tearing the living room to pieces. It was so surreal, I couldn't believe my eyes. Just a few weeks before, I was living in that home, creating memories, and calling it "my own." Now, it was being literally destroyed.

As if the stress of moving one more time wasn't enough, now I was hit with the sudden shock of seeing everything I knew to represent home being demolished before my very eyes.

The next day I came back and stood there for what seemed like hours, just trying to absorb this new crash of reality. I walked over to the man on the bulldozer, and asked, "What was it like for you to tear down this house?"

He answered, "It took me a whole day to tear it down. Normally, it takes me about two hours to demolish a house. Because this house was so well built, it took me about four times longer."

Each day I came back to watch the demolition process and the clearing away of rubble. Within a matter of days, I returned to the site, and walked around the property, which was about two acres. Every bit of metal, wood, and glass had been completely removed. You never would have known a house had been standing there. Just a few weeks before, I had been living in that house. Now it had completely disappeared, along with any vestige of remains.

Our herb gardens were gone. Mom's vegetable garden was gone. Teddy's back porch and yard were gone. The home that represented so many fond memories was gone. I reached into my pocket, feeling the key to the absent front door. "No need for a key anymore," I thought.

I couldn't help but stand there in a daze, and ask God, "Why?" My questions were just beginning. "God, why did you lead us to this house, only to have us move out, and then be subjected to the emotional trauma of seeing it torn down before our very eyes? I have to believe there's a message in this for me. If so, what is it You are trying to tell me? This is too bizarre not to have a higher purpose. Please reveal to me what it is You want me to know."

The illumination was immediate. "Veronica, I'm tearing down your house, a house that represents the order of your life. I'm completely destroying the old order of how you have lived and operated. There have been things that worked for you in the past that no longer are going to work for you. There were good things about that house, even beautiful things, things that were well-built, but the internal workings were broken. I'm completely sweeping away the house along with all its rubble. I'm going to build a brand new order in your life, and build something completely new. You don't even have need of keys. They won't work anymore. I am not a God of improvement. I am God who is Builder, and I build things to last. In order for Me to build something new in your life, I have to abolish the old structure and remove every last vestige of its remains. This is what I am doing in your life."

I didn't understand at the time the full ramifications of that revelation. However, I wanted to respond to the understanding I was given. I went back to the beach condo and got my mom. "Mom, God just showed me something about the spiritual meaning behind what just happened with the destruction of the Bay Colony home. I want to conduct a burial service, a rite-of-passage, so to speak, burying the old ways of doing things." We grabbed the dog and the key, and jumped back in the car to return to the property.

Two acres is a lot of land for one home on a tight neighborhood street. I wasn't quite sure where I wanted to bury the key to the old house. We started walking toward the crepe myrtle trees in the backyard. I was stunned as we walked across the site and didn't see one speck of what had been. It was as if the house had never there. "Someone did a really good job," Mom commented. As we walked around, I suddenly came upon an object that showed me that this was the place to bury the key.

"Mom!" I cried out. "Come over here! I can't believe this. As you can see, there isn't a shred of evidence that a house even existed here just a few days ago. On this entire property, there's only one thing left from the old house."

"What is it?" Mom asked.

"Look," I said, pointing in amazement. "It's a golf ball!" We stared at each other and smiled.

"Well, I'll be!" Mom said. One of her practice balls was sitting comfortably in the dirt. "Let's dig the hole right here."

I put the key in the hole and started the brief ceremony. "We are gathered here today . . ." Teddy-boy looked up at me after a brief sniffing spree. ". . . to proclaim the end to the old order of things. We receive the new order of things as You have planned and ordained for us today. We thank you for the wonderful memories we gathered in this home, and now we look to You for our next steps. Amen." "Amen," Mom repeated after me.

I wasn't quite sure what all of that meant, other than knowing how important it is to have closure over seasons and steps. Finding the golf ball was totally intriguing to me, and I wonder what that symbolized. I was soon to find out.

Moving Back to North Carolina

*W*hen my family came for Christmas, Mom and I had asked them about the possibilities of her moving back to her apartment in Fayetteville. We knew that it just wasn't going to work out long term for us to live together. That was fine for both of us. I was reluctant to see her return to North Carolina because I knew she wouldn't get the same degree of emotional and relational oversight I provided for her.

How do you know if you're making the right decision? I guess people make their decisions differently. However, I wanted to hear from God. If I could hear from Him, then I would know it would be the right decision, despite what I thought, or how it looked from the outside.

One of the ways I've learned to hear from God is through fasting. When I fast, I'm making myself more spiritually attuned to God and His ways. During a time of fasting, I was driving down the road in Virginia Beach. In front of me was a big truck. On the back flaps of his tires was imprinted the word "Fayetteville." "Fayetteville?" I thought.

I've lived in Virginia Beach for a total of fifteen years, and I have never seen that word on any sign in this city. I believed this was God's sign to me that it was His will and time for Mom to return to Fayetteville. My brother confirmed it.

Mom left for Fayetteville a few months before I had to be out of the condo. I wanted to enjoy the few months I had remaining to enjoy the beach and to regain some sense of my own self again.

It wasn't long before I was met with another big decision. Mom had struggled through another stint in the hospital after getting checked out by her doctor in Fayetteville. It happened during a time when my brother and his family were on vacation in the Bahamas. It turned out to be a false scare, but I had to go down to North Carolina to oversee her stay in the hospital.

One night while in Fayetteville, I decided to take a drive over to Pinehurst. The thought weighed heavily on my mind that maybe I should move to North Carolina myself. I was conflicted over the whole thing again. I made a commitment to Mom to see her through to the finish line, and she was not there yet. I also knew that if she was going to have any measure of a fullness of life, I would be the one to give it to her.

As I pulled into the center of the Village of Pinehurst, right at the main intersection of the town, I noticed a pretty Afro-American woman walking her toy American Eskimo Spitz across the street. I had never seen a toy version of my dog. All of sudden, Teddy-boy started barking his head off at this little doggie from his same breed. "Let's stop and meet your cousin, Teddy-boy!" The lady stopped to see where all the barking was coming from. Noticing another American Eskimo, she stopped, too. Right in the middle of the street, I stopped the car and got out!

I introduced myself and Teddy-boy, and met Brenda and her dog, Cody. Brenda and I immediately connected and became fast friends. I told her why I was in town, and she shared her story of leaving her company to launch off on a faith journey of her own. "Maybe God is leading you to take a leap of faith and move to Pinehurst," Brenda said after hearing an edited version of my story.

I knew that God has used my dog before to connect me with people to steer me, just as He used Teddy-boy to lead me to the woman who encouraged me to "just go home and love my mother." It was too bizarre not to think that here was another pivotal divine intersection of two lives coming together to encourage one another.

The next night I came back over to visit at the Pine Crest Inn. Sitting on the porch, one meets people from all over the world. "So what are you doing here?" the woman across from me asked.

"I'm considering moving here."

"Do you need a real estate agent?" she asked.

"Yes, I do," I said. "But I would just be renting. She recommended a real estate agent in town.

He had only one property in town that would take dogs, so I decided to check it out. Driving over to the house, I prayed, "Lord, I have moved too much and too often. If You want me to move here, I want You to take me directly to my new home. I don't want to explore. I want a straight shot to my next residence."

When I got to the house, it only took me a few minutes to know my prayer had been answered. Three bedrooms—one for me, one for Mom, and one for an office. Perfect size and affordable rent.

I went back to Virginia Beach, knowing that I would need some real closure to leave a place that had been home to me for so long. Moving to North Carolina would mean giving up my presidential scholarship worth about $40,000 to see Mom through. Having deferred it for a few years, I knew I would have to sacrifice my own career advancement again to make this leap of faith. My desire was to have more counsel and confirmation about my move. It was a very difficult decision.

One day while I was in the cafeteria at Regent University, I ran into the former president, Dr. Gyertson. He was a very wise man, and as many times as I frequented that place, I never saw him eating alone. I walked over to him and asked to visit with him for a few minutes. He was very gracious and invited me to join him for lunch. My questions were immediate. "Dr. Gyertson, I'm struggling between staying here in Virginia Beach where my coaching practice is just beginning to take off, and moving to North Carolina, where my aging mother is. She just moved back there several months ago. I promised to see her through to the end of her life."

His counsel was precious to me. "Your moving there would be based on the spiritual principle of honoring your parents. Even if it's hard for you, God will bless it. You can always have a distance relationship with the school and come back for seminars. I want to encourage you to move and fulfill your commitment to her. God will honor you."

His advice is what I needed to feel a release in my heart to go. I moved August 1, 2006. The meant I could keep my pledge to see Mom through down her final fairway.

The Final Fairway

*L*ittle did I know I would be moving to Pinehurst the same night of a hurricane. The torrential rains almost caused the driver of the moving truck to pull off the side of the road and delay his trip. Fortunately, as soon as he arrived, about midnight, the rain stopped just long enough for him to unpack the truck. At 2:00 a.m. that morning, I was in Harris Teeter, getting my storm supplies, as my neighbor back in Virginia Beach had urged me to do.

My time in Pinehurst proved to be much like the drive down—a continual struggle coupled with the most amazing grace when I needed it.

The first week I arrived in Pinehurst, I not only received help but some wonderful inspiration, too. One of the first persons I met was Jim Dodson. A nationally-acclaimed and award-winning golf author, Jim was giving a talk at the Pinehurst Literary luncheon that Saturday. He had written a wonderfully popular book called *Final Rounds,* which told the story of his relationship with his dying father, particularly on the golf course. I knew that Jim would understand the journey I was on with Mom. I just had to meet him—and I did.

I also wanted to establish the Grandma Open in Pinehurst. My dream was for it to be a lasting legacy in Mom's honor. It would also be an invitation to other families to create lasting legacies in their families. Bringing together the generations through golf while honoring the elderly became my new vision. Jim totally got the picture.

He graciously wrote a front page article on Mom and me within the first few months of our arrival in Pinehurst. I did my best to get the word out to the public, although I hardly knew anybody at the time.

Mom and I worked on our game together as the first Grandma Open in Pinehurst was slated to take place later that fall. It would be held at the practice loop of Pine Needles, the site of her first round of golf. The focus of the day was to provide an occasion for family enjoyment. It was about the relationships, not the scores.

Of course, we had to practice. One day Mom and I went out to play at Knollwood, a fun little public golf course. Driving down the fairway, we noticed an elderly lady coming in the opposite direction on the fairway next to us. We came prepared with some flyers to hand out, so I asked Mom, "Do you think we should drive over there and give this lady a flyer? We don't know her, but maybe she would like to play in our tournament."

"Of course!" Mom replied.

We made a quick right turn and hurried over to her. We quickly introduced ourselves and invited her to the upcoming tournament. We weren't sure what her response would be, and I thought I would have some real explaining to do about the event. She took one look at Mom and her eyes lit up. "Oh, I know who *you* are! You're the woman that was written about in the paper!" Mom's face lit up. She had never in her life been recognized as a celebrity before, but I could tell she was completely absorbed in the moment.

"You know me?" Mom asked, swelling with pride at the thought of being famous.

"Yes," the lady replied. "You're the host of the Grandma Open!"

I will never forget the look on Mom's face when she realized she was suddenly a public person, known as a golf celebrity. It was another eternal treasure I collected and put in my bag of memories. My mother had never been publicly honored in her life, and this was a slice of heaven for her—and me.

"Well, let's see you hit a golf ball," Mom said. The lady proceeded to hit a nice shot, and then turned to Mom.

"Now let's see *you* hit a golf ball. You're the famous one!" Mom looked at me a little sheepishly.

"Go ahead," I encouraged her. "Show the lady your stuff!" We drove back into our fairway. "Take out your three wood," I directed Mom, "and be sure to tee it up." We were on a par five hole, and Mom was taking her second shot.

She looked at me, a little nervous at the thought of someone watching her hit a ball and was feeling the pressure of having to perform in the moment. She marched over to the center of the fairway and teed up her ball. Seeing her trying so hard to look like an expert, I began to chuckle. Instead of teeing up to face toward the hole, Mom mistakenly teed up facing the opposite direction, towards the tee! "Mom!" I exclaimed. "You're teeing up the ball in the wrong direction. The hole is that way!" As I pointed in the opposite direction, Mom looked at me in total embarrassment. All three of us burst out laughing. I turned Mom around, teed up the ball for her, gave her a big hug, and said, "Now go!"

She took her characteristic waggle, made a big old backswing, swung down flush on the ball, and hit an absolutely dead perfect shot with her Patty Berg three wood, straight down the center of the fairway. It sailed a good 130 yards. Mom twirled around and looked at me with astonishment at the thought of performing under pressure. With her eyes almost bursting out her head, she let out a big shout, "I did it!"

"Mom, that was a fantastic shot! You did it!" The lady smiled, waved goodbye, and promised she would help get the word out to her group.

I'll never forget that perfect shot and the look on Mom's face when she executed a perfect swing. So often we think it's the big shots or events in life that mean the most. Like connecting spirit to spirit at the tip of the Atlantic Ocean in a canoe, this was another in-the-diamonds moment when Mom and I connected in spirit. Once I was become aware that lasting memories are created by "in the moment" experiences, it was easier for me to relish them, cherish them, and add them to my heart's storehouse. I also knew that it was vital to be intentional about the memory collection. It's so easy to let the days and years pass by. Like my neighbor said, "When they're gone, they're gone." I knew there was an endpoint to experiencing life with my mother. I just didn't know when.

The turnout for the Grandma Open was small. We had just a handful of families, but the experience was great. My friend Troy and his wife, Marie, came down from Virginia Beach to help out. Troy, a budding photographer, captured some splendid pictures of the day. It was the *Guidepost* article that led him to contact me, and both his and Marie's friendship has meant a great deal to me. They became like a surrogate brother and sister coming alongside me, to see me through Mom's passing. Mom became a surrogate mother to them, too. One of the pictures Troy took during the day was a perfect photo of my brother, mom, and me standing on the tee at Pine Needles. The light behind us was particularly illuminated. It was a real shot-of- joy moment.

The biggest hit of the day was a giant-sized Hershey's chocolate bar that we gave away as one of the main prizes. All the kids vied for that it. I also gave Mom a "Champion of the Heart" award. Peggy Kirk Bell took a picture with Mom and her award. Mrs. Bell herself was struggling with health problems. Mom was now ninety. Mrs. Bell was in her mid-eighties. Both were champions in their own right and cut out of the same cloth. I could tell that Mom inspired Peggy with her health, and Peggy inspired Mom. Two champs in their own right, now fighting a new kind of championship—to remain strong until the end.

More memorable experiences lay ahead.

A shot of joy at the Grandma Open with Mom and Mike

Legacy Building: Remembering the Moments

*T*he next year of living in Pinehurst was a combination of collecting memories and being Mom's caregiver through her continued debilitation. Her heart condition kept her from walking long distances, a trait she was noted for, even in her old age. It seemed that each month her endurance waned, and she struggled to do the things that had always been easy for her.

At times the weight of taking care of her almost did me in. With little support, and with only a part-time job, I felt constant financial pressure. The champion in me was committed to seeing Mom through, but at what expense? I had to let a lot of things go, like my own relationships, goals, and dreams. The flipside of paying that price was the extraordinary satisfaction I had when Mom and I ventured out and experienced life-enhancing moments together. This always confirmed that it was worth the price I was paying.

One time I took Mom along with me for a speaking engagement I had at the local Professional Women's Network luncheon. I was speaking on the process of authentic change. As before, Mom introduced me. When the audience saw us together, they got the biggest kick out of the mother-daughter duo standing before them. "I felt so important," Mom told me later. "All those ladies wanted to talk to me afterward." I realized just how rare it is for a mother and daughter to team up and flow together in any area, especially as adults. I was so pleased that the fruit of my labor was evident to others, even strangers.

Putting Mom in new atmospheres to see other sides of her come forward was a joy to behold. So much of her identity had been tied to her being a worker that I rarely saw the purely feminine side of her emerge. The atmosphere of women gathered together brought out this aspect.

During that last year, her two closest friends from Virginia Beach, Wanda and Calene, came to visit us. What was special about Wanda and Calene is that they were shared friends. I was so far apart in age from Mom that having two women friends who bridged the gap made it easier for me to relate to Mom. They could be both my friend and Mom's friend at the same time.

Sometimes I think that adult children of aging parents feel they have to do all the caregiving alone. There are many things that aging parents can't open up about with their own children, but they can with other people. I had no problem sharing Mom with my friends. It brought a lot of positive energy from others to the table, and I needed that. Mom needed it too.

Calene was especially close to Mom. She would often comment, "I just think women your mother's age are so important in our culture, and they are a dying breed. We need to learn from their wisdom and their experience."

One morning while they were visiting me, we made a wonderful breakfast. Of course, Mom had to be the one cooking her famous quiche. We set the table with our fine china. Normally Mom would be quick to get up from the table and wash the dishes, but as got into a discussion about relationships and women, she sat there spellbound. For over an hour, she just sat and listened. Although she didn't say a word, you could tell she was soaking up every bit of the exchange. I can't even remember what we were talking about specifically, but at the end of it all, Mom got up and announced, "Well, this was a very enlightening morning! I learned so much from all of you! Thank you very much."

I had to chuckle. Mom was ninety, seriously ill, but still

learning and curious about life. So much of her attention had always been on serving and doing—to see her light up in a conversation about personal growth and relationships was a real surprise to me. If Calene and Wanda hadn't come, I never would have known that part of Mom's soul existed and was very much alive.

One night we had a girls' night out. I've mentioned that Mom and I had exchanged roles to a degree, with my becoming her mother, and she, my daughter. Interestingly, along with that came a shift in our physical shapes. I used to be thin and got heavier. Mom used to be heavy and was now thin! I had bought a beautiful Hawaiian-looking dress—very sexy—that I couldn't fit into any more. Guess who wore it to dinner? Mom! Here was my ninety-year-old mother wearing my uptown dress to dinner! After we ate, we took a picture of the four of us girls. It continues to be a source of inspiration to me even now, as I keep it on my bathroom counter.

I also kept my cousins apprised of Mom's condition, letting them know around Easter time in 2007 that I didn't think she had long to live. My cousins Wally, Johnnie, and their families came down for Easter from Pittsburgh to visit Mom one more time.

During the weekend, the annual Stoneybrook Horse Race was taking place at the Carolina Horse Park. It was frigid outside, but we all wanted to go. Every decision Mom and I made, we did as a team. That morning around the dining room table, with everyone present, I asked, "Mom do you want to go to the race? Are you up to it?" I trusted her response. "Yes," she replied, "I want to go." So we went—in faith, once again, on another adventure.

When we arrived at the track, we didn't calculate how far away we would have to park. Just as we made the turn into the parking lot, we saw a golf cart whiz by. I caught the driver's attention. "Hey! Can you stop for a moment and take an old lady across the street? She has a heart condition."

"No problem. Hop in!" Mom and I climbed into the golf cart and were chauffeur-driven to our spot at the race.

My friend, Teresa, had a company sponsored spot. When Mom got cold, she sat in Teresa's pickup truck. It was the perfect compromise between keeping Mom warm and letting her come to the race. Outside, we all took bets on who was going to win. Cousin Wally raked in a stack of dollars. Mom was just thrilled to be with us. After the race, the man with the golf cart took Mom back to the car. I was always amazed at how things worked out when we stepped out in faith to go on adventure.

Besides our big family event, our favorite moments were those captured in speaking together. Every time I had the chance to bring Mom along with me for a speaking engagement, I did. While her job had been to introduce me, which she did on numerous occasions, I thought it was time to take her speaking expertise to the next level. In late November, I was invited to speak at a college campus ministry at the University of North Carolina at Chapel Hill. Since my topic was "Fresh Fuel for the Finish Line," I thought it would be appropriate for Mom to have five minutes to speak about finishing strong herself. Although I would be focusing on academics and finals, it was completely in sync for her to talk about how she was finishing strong in her life.

Charles Kiefer, the head of the group, invited us to dinner, warmly welcoming us to campus. When the time came, he introduced Mom. "Before Veronica comes and speaks, we have a very special guest with us tonight who is going to say a few words and introduce Veronica."

The students cheered and clapped as they saw an elderly woman get up before them. "Hello!" Mom beamed. "My name is Mildred Karaman and I am ninety-one years old!" As she continued, smiling exuberantly, the students cheered and clapped even more. "Tonight I'm going to talk to you about finishing strong. The key to finishing strong is HARD WORK!" As Mom went on her schpeil, sharing a message that I'm sure those students didn't want to hear——about working hard—they were captivated by her.

At one point, she got so wound up that she completely left her notes and starting talking from her spirit. "Yeah, these doctors, they gave me six months to live. Well, here I am, seven years later. I'm still here. Where the hell are they?" The students cracked up, cheering her on all the more.

All of a sudden, she realized she had strayed from the page and didn't know how to get back to her subject. "Oh, excuse me. I'm a little nervous here," she confessed as she tried with obvious embarrassment to return to her notes. "Well, don't forget, the key to success and finishing strong is hard work! Now here's my favorite golf partner, my daughter, Veronica Karaman." The class clapped wildly as Mom sat down and I got up. "Okay, let's hear it for Mom!" I exclaimed with glee.

"Go Mom!" the students applauded again. I looked at her. In that moment, she was on top of the world—full of joy and satisfaction about what she had just accomplished in her public speaking exploit. Here she was, walking down her final fairway, hitting life shots into the next stratosphere. Her talk at Chapel Hill would be her last one.

I had one more speaking engagement to college students, this one with Duke students. I debated whether or not to take Mom with me. It was a Sunday afternoon, the day after the Reindeer Fun Run. I knew she was tired, so I decided in was best to leave her home. "Now Mom, you just rest. Don't do anything while I'm gone, but just rest. Got that?" She promised me she would rest.

As I made the hour and a half drive to Durham by myself, I thought about leaving Mom at home. I wanted so badly to take her with me, but I knew she couldn't make the trip. All during my time in the car, I felt an incredibly deep love for my mother. What had started with hatred in my heart for her seven years before was totally transformed into the deepest well of love I have ever known for another human being. It was a supernatural change born out of a partnership with God that would not quit. Perhaps I needed to experience that kind of unconditional love because of what was going to transpire in just a few hours.

The Alarm

*A*fter my speech, I checked the voicemail on my cell phone. "Veronica, this is Mom. I think I'm dying. I can't breathe. I was afraid to call you, but please come home."

It was the call I never wanted to get. I immediately called her, as two hours had passed since I'd received the frightening message. Mom answered. "I was afraid to move because I thought I would have a heart attack and die, but I picked up the phone."

"Mom, are you okay?" I questioned in panic.

"I'm still here, just trying to be still."

"I'll be right home. Just take it easy," I assured her.

I jumped in my car and raced home. Once in the door, I saw Mom lying back in the living room chair. "What happened?" I asked.

"I was coming up the back porch steps and all of a sudden I couldn't breathe. I was afraid to move, thinking I was going to die if I took another step." My gut knew better.

"Were you working outside? Did you go into your turbo-cleaning mode while I was gone? I told you just to rest!" She looked down at the floor. "Mom! You were cleaning weren't you?"

"Yes," she sheepishly confessed.

"You did this to yourself!" I said, both scolding her and hugging her at the same time

I immediately called the doctor, and explained what had happened. All he could say is that it was going to get worse and there was nothing they could do. I could bring her into the hospital again to drain the fluid out of her lungs, but at some point, it was a hopeless cause. Her heart was shutting down. It was our call.

Not knowing what to do, we decided together that she would rest for a few days. I was scared not knowing the future and how much longer she had. I just wanted to be with her as much as I could and make the right decision.

A few days later as I was sitting by the bed, Mom looked at me and said, "Veronica, if it weren't for you, I would have died years ago. It's because of all your good care and all that you have done for me that I am still here. The doctors gave me six months, and here I've lasted seven years." Tears began to well up.

"I know, Mom. It's been quite the ride, hasn't it? You're quite the trooper," I commended her.

"*You* are the trooper!" she said. I hugged her as I assured her, "Mom, I'm going all the way to the finish line with you. Whatever it takes. We're going there together." Then I left the room crying.

Several days later, when it was obvious she wasn't getting any better, I decided to admit her to the hospital. They drained her lungs of fluid, and after a time of good rest, she came home.

At Thanksgiving, my friends Troy and Marie came down again to visit. Another priceless moment occurred as we sat around the dining room table talking. Because Marie took such an interest in Mom, asking her questions about her life, Mom's spirit broke free. "Just a minute, Marie." Mom got up from the table, went into her room, and brought back her wedding album. "Let me show you all about my wedding and my husband." For the next hour, Mom poured out her life to Marie.

"Troy," I said, wanting to capture the moment, "Let's videotape this. This is the perfect moment to capture Mom's story while she isn't self-conscious." He and I set up the video camera and caught much of Mom's story on tape. It was a precious time. I was so grateful that God had sent Troy and Marie into our lives as surrogate family members. Troy contributed his talent as a photographer, and Marie had such a gift of "taking interest in people" that she drew out of Mom information I never could have. Their friendship was a gift in so many ways.

After dinner that night, we decided to watch *The Sound of Music*. We arranged the comfortable chairs in theater style and made popcorn. To make it official, I created theater tickets and asked Mom to pass them out. "Gee, if I knew you were going to charge me for the ticket, I wouldn't have come!" she exclaimed. We all chuckled and enjoyed our movie, which would be Mom's last.

A few days later, I phoned her doctor to check in again. I wasn't able to reach him, but the doctor on call took my call. "Doctor," I asked, "I'm wondering how long my mother has to live. She as a severe aortic stenosis with congestive heart failure." As I laid out all her symptoms, I asked him to be upfront with me.

"When someone has those symptoms, I would give them about six weeks to live." I thanked him for his candor and hung up—stunned, but somewhat relieved that a doctor was real with me.

I appreciated Mom's physician, but every time I asked him how long he thought she had to live, it was always, "Well, she could go tomorrow or last a year." I needed more insight than that, and I was grateful to have stumbled upon this man who gave me the information I needed.

Approaching the Final Green

*W*hen I grasped the finality of Mom's life and the timing of her having only a few weeks left, I called my brother. "Mike, the doctor just told me Mom has only up to six weeks to live based on his judgment of her condition. I think we need to get the family together one final time while she's still lucid." It was a strained conversation, as my brother and his family didn't see eye to eye with me about Mom's care. They certainly didn't understand my quest with her. However, I needed to give them this information and invite them to gather around her

This was early December of 2007, after the Reindeer Fun Run memory and her visit to the hospital. Mom had a sense that her time was short. We had a conversation one day about inviting the family over for dinner. "I think we should have a pierogie party," I suggested. "Remember having my girlfriends over about a month ago? We had a great time all standing around the kitchen island, each making our own pierogies. What do you think?"

Mom thought for a moment and replied, "How about my just making a roast?" As we pondered the evening's purpose, I said, "I think we need to do something that involves everyone participating."

"Okay," she said. "I'll make pierogies. After all, they are the family favorite."

I called my brother and asked him and his family to come over. We weren't quite sure what the gathering would be like, but Mom and I had done everything by faith up until this point, so we weren't going to be afraid of one more adventure. Mom went to town the next few days putting together all the ingredients for the dinner. At one point, I was a little concerned because what was supposed to be just a simple dinner kept becoming more complicated. Mom didn't know how to just "make a simple dinner." She had to go all out, getting out the good china and everything that went along with a first-class spread.

Having conversation was not always an easy thing for my family, so I decided to buy some red felt material and white felt snowflakes. If things got a little rough, we could always put together a fun craft to break the ice.

When the time came for the dinner, Mom was already worn out from all her preparations, and I admittedly felt bad about making the choice I did. A roast would have been much easier. We began the evening with cutting out a Christmas apron for Mom, and Elise, my younger niece, cut out several red hearts. We glued the snowflakes and hearts on Mom's red apron, and it was a nice "gift in the making for her." The funny part about the pierogies was the flour. We didn't know that it was rancid. When we put the pierogies in the boiling water, they came unraveled. We wanted to create a memory, but not one of bad flour spoiling our meal!

Just when we thought we wouldn't have anything to eat, Mike came to the rescue. "Give me a frying pan," he commanded, "and a lot of butter." Always resourceful, he put the ailing pierogies in the frying pan and greased it up good. "Let's add some fried onions in here. That will help the taste!" In no time at all, he had rescued our failed attempt to put together one final family meal. We all had a good laugh about it.

After dinner, we took a family picture, but then Mom started to cough horribly. The stress was too much for her, and she began to fade fast. My family said their goodbyes, and I quickly put Mom to bed. I had to prop her up because she couldn't breathe lying down. I didn't know what to do at this point, so I told her, "Look, I'm going to leave this bell right here. If you need it, just ring it, and I'll come right away."

Ringing of the Bell

The following morning at about 6:00 a.m., I heard what I had hoped never to hear—the ringing of that bell. I ran into Mom's room and saw that she was having a tough time breathing. "Call 911," she bellowed. "I've had the worse Charley horse."

About fifteen minutes later, the paramedics arrived and whisked her off to the hospital. Fortunately, one of the paramedics gave her Lasix on the way over to drain the fluid from her lungs. Fortunately, her blood pressure was sustained. I thought she was getting better, but later in the day she got weaker.

I went back over at about 5:00 pm. Going into the hospital, I met a black minister and his wife. They introduced themselves as Charles and Barbara. I asked him to come pray for my mother. He was delighted to. When they came into the room, they were amazed at how young Mom looked. He opened up the Bible to a wonderful Psalm and preached a Sunday sermon right there for her. He testified as to how God had healed him of fatal skin cancer. Then he began to sing "Amazing Grace" over her life. At one point, the "faith" message became too much for her.

"All right. You did a good job. Now you can stop," she said.

"My, we have a pistol here," the preacher responded. "We've got to pray. You have got to have faith to the finish and not give up hope." We gathered hands and prayed that Mom would go on God's time and not her own.

It was an amazing moment. A total stranger had spoken to

Mom's spirit and commanded her faith to be strong until the end. I thought this was the end. So did she. We called Mike to come to the hospital. When he arrived, we had a nice conversation. Mom cried and said her goodbyes. It was a tender moment as we held hands and prayed over her. "I have two wonderful children. Veronica did a great job helping me out. Tell the girls I love them." My brother commented on how there was nothing wrong with any of my mother's parts except her heart. Pretty amazing.

At one point, Mom simply said, "Well, thanks for coming. I'm tired now and I'm going to sleep." And just like that, she closed her eyes and called it a day. Mike and I just looked at one another like, as if to say, "That's a new one."

After we said goodbye and walked down the hallway, I turned around to go back to Mom's room. She was still awake. "I'm glad you stayed, Veronica," she said softly.

I was crying as I poured my heart out to her. "Mom, I want you to stay, but if you want to go, I give you permission to go. Do you want to go?"

"Yes," was her answer. "I want to go."

"Well, okay then." I wasn't sure if I should leave, although I was exhausted and felt I had the closure to go home.

I kissed her on the forehead and headed down to the purple elevators. Though I cried all the way home, I felt strength in my heart. I also felt the strength of people's prayers and the grace of God with me.

Driving home I prayed, "God, I pray Mom makes it through the night."

Hospice

To my surprise, Mom made it through the night. Her breathing was much better, and the doctor released her from the hospital a few days later. She was very weak, but concerned about her appearance, as always. We talked about the handsome doctor that I had a crush on, Dr. Hagas. Too bad he was married!

Once we were home, the calls started coming in to set up hospice. A man with oxygen tanks came over and set up a big unit in her room. Teddy-boy was too afraid to get on the bed with all the hoses hanging around, but he eventually became comfortable with the new setup.

Pat, the worker from Pinehurst Hospice, arrived and was very pleasant. And Mom like her because she was Polish, too. They even exchanged a few words in Polish. I came to realize just how helpful hospice was. It's not only for people who are at the end of their lives. It's also for those with terminal illnesses who need help in the home. We went over a zillion details, and for the first time in this process, I felt empowered.

The hospice included a lot of support with various visits scheduled during the week. Terri, her nurse, was terrific. She was one person Mom would listen to and laugh with. Terri had asked for special permission to be Mom's nurse, as she was only supposed to be her intake person.

All this left me with a sense of both hope and pressure. It's a whole new level of responsibility and adjustment to have someone permanently in your home. It was hard for me to think about my own job and forward progress.

At dinner Mom and I shared a hoagie. Teddy sat on the bed. It was another exhausting day. Later I watched the Suzy Orman show. She was talking about women using their power to control their own destiny with money. She spoke about how women have a dysfunctional relationship with money, and how we really need to put ourselves first when it comes to money. It really spoke to me about how I had allowed myself to be the sacrificial lamb when it came to taking care of Mom. I had drained a big savings account and I needed help to share the financial responsibility for her current care. I talked to Mom about this, and she agreed that I should ask my brother to help. We each felt good about making the request.

Before I called it a day, I walked the dog. As I looked up, the most amazing stars were out, big and bright, and calling me up into a higher reality. In my journal I wrote, "As much as my reality is consumed with a dying woman, my mother, there is a big world out there. God is there and reminding me that He holds my life and times in His hands. I love looking up into the Pinehurst sky. The air is clean and still—fills up my lungs with fresh oxygen just like that tank puts fresh oxygen into Mom's lungs. I suck it in and bask in the wonder of God's creation. The stars are like a zillion friends, reminding me that support is there. The world is much bigger than my world. I am reminded that at any moment God can drop-ship provision from the big world into my little world. And He did just that today, with someone sending me a $500 check, totally unexpected. It meant so much to me. Thank you, God! Please keeping reminding me of Your greatness. I'm exhausted and experiencing a strange mix of strength and weakness, tears and joy."

I often found my connections to nature to be a source of renewal for me. Often I would take the dog and go to the Pinehurst Harness Track. There's a dirt track at the back, one mile around. I liked going there because my jogging progress can be easily measured. Teddy and I went four times around the track, he racing me, me racing him, except of course when he caught wind of a squirrel. Then he was gone. I never thought I would welcome the smell of horse poop as much as I did. That smell represented freshness, simplicity, connection to the earth. When my world is overwhelming, God's world is grounding and healing.

In just a few days, however, the caregiving became more than I could bear.

Letting Go

The next few days became so overwhelming, I felt like I was having a heart attack emotionally. The burden of taking care of Mom full time became too much for me. I was feeling the weight of the world crashing in on me. In so many ways I saw my mother in me—always pushing to the extreme, thinking I can do more than I actually can.

I knew if things were going to work, my brother would have to help me out financially and help provide for companion services. I finally got up the courage to send the email I'd written a few days before, requesting his assistance. Then, out of the blue, my girlfriend, Cynthia, called.

"Veronica, I've had you on my mind all day. I know when that happens, God is wanting me to call you. What is going on?" I explained to her how I felt I was losing myself in the process of taking care of Mom, and that there was no way I could carry both the financial and emotional burdens. "Just call your brother and let him have the responsibility of your mom," she said. "He's in a much better position to take care of her. Just do it."

After emailing him, he wrote back and said he would be more than willing to pick her up the next day, which was Friday. When I called him to work out details, I burst out crying. "I can't do this." I kept waffling on my decision, feeling the tug of war going on in my heart of my wanting to care for Mom and at the same time, needing to take care of my own needs.

After my crying spell, I knew I would need assistance in communicating with my brother and following through with the decision to transfer Mom back to her apartment in Fayetteville. I called my pastor's wife, Trudy. Sobbing, as if I were the one who was dying, I cried, "I need help."

"I'll be right over," Trudy said.

One of the calmest people I know, she was terrific. When I asked her what I should do, she replied, "Call your brother back and tell him to come pick up your mother this afternoon. Don't wait another day. Just do it. Do you want me to get on the phone with you?"

"Yes," I whimpered. So together we called my brother and worked out the details of his coming to pick up Mom.

While I was getting her ready for her departure, she asked me to help put her curlers in her hair. Now Mom's hair was sacred territory. Not even the most intimate of mates could touch her hair, so I knew that this gesture meant entering into a deeper relationship with her.

Her curlers were of ancient days. They were green and yellow and made of hard plastic. They looked like they had been through World War II. I tried getting her to use some soft plastic ones, but they weren't stoic enough. "Doesn't feel like my hair is wet. Be sure to wet it! And don't put too much hair on one curler. Make sure it's tight." I felt like I was obeying the orders of a general. "You're not doing it right," Mom complained.

"Mom," I responded, "this isn't rocket science."

"Why are you standing in front of me to curl my hair?" Why aren't you standing in back of me?" Mom fumed.

"I don't know. I have good leverage from here," I explained. Once I got through the verbal challenge and finished her hair, she took her mirror and examined my first hair-curling effort. "You did a fine job! Better than I could!" I could have smacked her!

It touched me that she would let me help her with her hair. Of course, she had to be presentable to the world, even if she was just going home to bed. She had to look good, even if she was dying.

Before Mike arrived, I sat on her bed, and helped her put a band aid around her bleeding toe. "What did you do?" I asked as blood was dripping on my beige carpet.

"I wanted to pull this piece of my nail off. It was dry." The skin around her big left toe was bleeding profusely through the gobs of zinc oxide she had put on." Once I got the band aid securely on her toe, we had a few minutes of waiting for my brother to arrive.

Knowing it would be the last time she would be in my house, she left the key to the front door on the little stand by the door. It hit me hard, knowing that she knew that she wouldn't be coming back.

Through the years of diligently working on communicating with my mother—the last seven years in particular—we found an arrangement that worked quite well. When she had trouble expressing herself, I would say, "Repeat after me . . ." and she would repeat my words. Then she would get on a roll, find her own voice, and take it from there. It seemed I developed quite a knack for knowing what she was feeling but had trouble expressing at first.

"Okay, repeat after me," I said. First, I held out my hand as if to give her a papal blessing. Likewise, she held out her hand toward me. "I bless you my daughter, and I release you to live a life of happiness, prosperity, and goodness."

She took it from there, ". . . and to be happily married and to live your own life. I bless you!" We hugged, and I felt the blessing of my mother enter my bones. It was life-giving. It also felt as if everything that needed to be wrapped up—like a Christmas present all neatly tied up in a big bow—had just taken place. There was nothing more to say or do. My race with Mom was finished and had ended in a great victory, with her releasing me and giving me her blessing. Even though she was leaving my home and had yet to leave the earth, everything was fulfilled and reconciled between us. Now it was my brother's turn.

When Mike arrived, he brought some poinsettias with him.

They had been sitting in his car for several days and needed water, but even so, I appreciated them. It was time for Mom to say goodbye to her Teddy-boy. "Give Mommy a kiss," I told him. He ran over and kissed Mom with many licks.

We got Mom in the car and loaded up all the oxygen tanks. Fortunately, the hospice company let us take the tanks to Fayetteville for the weekend without charge. After Mike climbed into the car, I hugged him. "Thank you for taking Mom," I said, and gave him a kiss.

"We'll take good care of her," he replied. That was the assurance I needed. Off they drove with Mom breathing with the help of her portable oxygen unit.

I first thought there would be a hole in my heart when I closed the door and was left alone for the first time in weeks. However, the opposite happened. I felt the most wonderful sense of freedom, a freedom like I've never known. I had fully released my mother, and I could now pursue my own life without impediment. "So this is what the journey has been all about this year," I said to myself. "I now have the freedom and confidence to enter the world as my own person. I'm only forty-eight! I'm thankful that I have good genes and a heart that's ten years younger than my age."

For a few moments I basked in the freedom of wholeness. I knew that for years I had been trapped in the kaka of struggling to be released from my mother's hold, but this was the first time I had stepped beyond the confusion and torment of the relationship that never was, and now is. As I had learned before from Henry Cloud's book, *Boundaries*, you cannot separate from someone you've never bonded with. Separation must come first from a bonded place. Having so fully bonded with my mother, I was now able to separate. My cup was full. We had reached the eighteenth hole—the finishing hole—and felt the joy of a journey completed. It wasn't without whiffed shots, hitting in the hazard, or needing a zillion mulligans, but we reached the finish line together. The ball dropped. The cup was filled. All that was left was the finishing touches to her release to glory.

The Final Spin:
Further Reconciliation

*R*eleasing my mother into the care of my brother and sister-in-law, with whom I had a tenuous relationship, was both scary and freeing. I had assumed responsibility for Mom's care for such a long time, that to so quickly turn it over to another family member was monumental. I wasn't emotionally prepared for the transfer of authority to my brother.

The following day I called Mom. She was in the middle of breakfast. "They brought breakfast to me in bed! Nancy is fantastic and gave me my medications. I'll call you later," she said. She was still feeling very weak, but we all sensed that she would be more comfortable in her own apartment.

After my call, I felt an extraordinary peace. As Mom was getting ready to enter eternity, I felt ready for a new season in my life. I still had a huge battle to forge through the next week, however, which would be Mom's last.

The following day, a Sunday, I called Mike. He said Mom wasn't doing well, that she had major issues with breathing. It sounded urgent, so right after church I drove straight over to Fayetteville.

They had given her some morphine to knock her out—knocked out she was. I was very concerned that hospice hadn't come yet. Mike and Nancy were doing a great job, but I felt that hospice should have been on the scene to lift the medical burden from them. As I walked into Mom's room, I saw two new lovely pajama sets hanging from the door—Nancy's gifts to her. I appreciated her kind expression.

When I got home, I spoke with Rev. Charles, the minister I'd met on the way to the hospital. I shared my concern that she should be getting hospice care, or at least my family should know it was available to them. He gave me some sound advice. "Veronica, the fact that your mom has had to totally depend upon your brother and sister-in-law is God's way to complete things between them. That wouldn't have happened if hospice was involved." His words gave me peace. It is always so amazing to get a heavenly perspective on things.

I knew that God cared about the entire family, not just me. I had been with Mom for so long, I had to believe that God was wanting to wrap things up with the rest of the family. My prayer became, "Lord, don't let Mom go one second too soon. Let everything be wrapped up with everyone."

The following day I went over to see Mom because she wanted to tell me something, saying it in a way that made me think it was going to be something profound. But as it turned out, she just wanted to give me her food stamp card! For her that was a big thing, so I accepted it as such.

She also wanted to call her niece, Patty. Mom was too weak to get on the phone, so I made the call and played interpreter. "What do you want to say to Patty, Mom?" She teared up.

"Tell her I love her, and I hope to see her soon." Patty burst out crying, I started to cry, and so did Mom. I wanted to keep her from getting too emotional, so we ended the conversation there. "I'm glad I said that!" Mom said, proud of herself for expressing her heart. Apparently there was something she had wanted to make amends with her niece. I began to understand that when people are dying, they need to reconcile things with their loved ones before they go.

After sharing some vital information about Mom's thyroid medication with my family, I left, proud of myself for being able to turn the whole hospice thing over to them.

More Wrap Ups

*T*he week Mom spent back at her own home was a huge stressor for me. My family didn't understand my need to be with my mother. I felt such an urgency every day to be there, and quite frankly, I didn't understand it either. I should have sat down and talked with them to reach some measure of understanding, but the tension was so great that I kept getting pushed away, and I didn't know what to do. At a time when family should rally around a dying person, I felt cut off.

Yet in God's mercy, He sent me some backups. Our mutual friend, Calene and her daughter, Xandria, came to visit us. Calene wanted to say goodbye to Mom and comfort me in my grief. She asked if she could treat me to a visit to the Pinehurst Spa. I wasn't exactly in the mood to go to a spa, although getting some kind of treatment was exactly what I needed after a week of overwhelming emotions and physical exhaustion. As much as Calene's timing didn't seem to be right, I decided not to control the situation but invite her to come, trusting God in His plans and purposes. She drove down from Virginia Beach, bringing her daughter, Xandria.

When Calene arrived, she and I went to the spa. I had a pedicure, and afterward, we laughed and prayed and cried over Mom. At dinner, Xandria, a senior at the University of Virginia and an exceptional, godly young woman, updated me on her life and college progress. Everything she spoke about was a fruit and

162

fulfillment of the academic and life coaching I had done with her over a year before.

We had an awesome time of prayer and decided to have communion with Mom when we met with her. On the way, we stopped to get blueberry sparkling lemonade, communion elements, and candy trays. Mom was weak when we arrived and a bit slow-talking but lucid. She was so glad to see her dog, Teddy-boy. Her face lit up to receive his kisses.

Immediately, Calene connected with my nieces, Rachel and Elise, and I introduced the girls to Xandria. Then, Calene, Xandria, and I went in to visit Mom. She was sitting up in bed and happy to see Calene. We broke bread and prayed, attuned to the sacred and solemn moment of communion, but it wasn't until Calene invited my nieces into the room that the atmosphere changed.

"Let's break out the blueberry sparkling lemonade and toast Mom!" I proposed. Everyone's countenance lit up as the mood changed from one of somberness to lightness. Elise and Rachel gathered the glasses, each of them a different size and shape. The one that stood out was the big wine glass with the Jewish star painted in different colors over the surface of the glass. "This one is for Mom," said. We filled up the glasses and gathered around her. It was a precious and intimate moment. "Let's each toast to Mom," I suggested as the spontaneous moment turned into one of destiny and spirit-to-spirit connection.

"I want to toast Mom for her radiant beauty. For her skin and all the ways she defies the odds of what a ninety-one year old woman should look like!"

"I wanted to say that!" said Rachel.

"I want to toast Mildred for her perseverance. Whatever she started to do or set her mind to do, she followed it through. Because of you, Mildred, I'm a better person, wife, mother, and believer," offered Calene.

"I want to toast Grandma's walks to Westwood Shopping Center," Elise stated.

"Yes, the athlete in her," I affirmed.

"I want to toast to Grandma's wit."

"Yes, yes," everyone agreed. "Here's to Grandma's amazing wit, even now!" Mom's eyes lit up. I forget what Xandria toasted to, but we were all in good cheer, saying, "Hear ye, hear ye!" as we clicked glasses and drank the sparkling blueberry lemonade. It was a rare moment of deep connection and joy with my family. Calene then affirmed my calling and profession as a life coach, sharing with the girls how I had helped guide her daughter on the right course of self-discovery for her life and wholeness.

I had also bought a dozen white roses at the Fresh Market. I picked up the vase and handed Mom a rose for each of us. It was her turn salute us. I can't remember what she said to each one individually, but something along the lines of "Rachel, you're the best granddaughter I could ever have. Elise, you're the best granddaughter I could ever have. Veronica, you're the best daughter I could ever have. Calene, you're the best friend I could ever have." I forget what she said to Xandria. It was a beautiful moment. We all laughed approvingly at each tribute.

After that we held hands and prayed. I opened up and asked Calene to close. After I prayed, there was silence. Never in a million years did I expect what would come next. All of sudden, my very staunch Roman Catholic mother, whom I could not force to pray out loud with me ever, began with no prodding whatsoever to pray. "Dear Jesus, thank you for this time. Thank you for all the ways my family has cared for me. Thank you for Rachel and Elise. I hope to get to know them better. Amen."

I was stunned. It was one of the most profound moments of my life, to see my mother pray from her heart so honesty, openly, and with the innocence of a child. It made me realize that someone's flesh may die, but her spirit continues to breathe fresh life no matter how old she is. I knew this moment was another gift to me. Not only was our gathering another shot of joy, but it was a special fruit given to me for all the times I'd spent praying in my mother's presence. She was growing spiritually, even up to a few days before her death.

Calene closed the prayer and exhorted us all, saying, "Mildred's time is determined by God. It is in His timing that she will go. It's all in the Lord's hands." It was a wonderful exchange of love and fellowship.

Final Days

The next day I went over to visit Mom. She was sitting up in her chair but was very weak. I called Roberta, her niece, and put them on the phone together. Roberta burst out crying—and so did Mom. I took the phone away from her to keep her from getting too emotionally drained. It was her chance to say goodbye to her other niece whom she'd visited quite often in past years.

Then we watched Oprah with Teddy-boy who jumped in bed with us and gave Mom some kisses. Nancy prepared lasagna, and Mom ate a good bit.

I wanted to be close to Mom, so I crawled in bed with her and held her hand. I felt around the covers and found her mirror, which she had hidden. Even dying in bed, she had to make sure she looked good! Her wit was also intact. "Pull the bottom of the cover down a little bit more. It has to line up with the cover at the other end. You know me . . . everything has to be perfect." She went on, "My mouth is so dry. Wish I had a good beer right now!"

"Veronica," she said, "I thought I was sleeping and something or someone was tapping me on the shoulder. I woke up and nobody was there. I think they were spirits or something. It scared me."

Before I left I went into her room and prayed over her and anointed her door with oil. Then I prayed over her and asked, "Mom, do you have peace in your heart—peace that you are going to heaven?"

She replied, "Yes, and I have the keys, too." I wasn't expecting that answer!

I was so glad I'd been able to pray with Calene that morning before I visited Mom. She encouraged me as a Christian woman to meditate on the Scriptures so that the Word of God would be in the CENTER of my heart. It's interesting that we can keep the Scripture in our hearts, but it can still be on the periphery. The greatest power in golf lies in hitting the ball in the center of the clubhead. I'd never seen this analogy before, but it is true. We need to keep the Word in the center of our hearts if our lives are to demonstrate the greatest power.

My swing-thought for the day was, "Stay strong for Mom." I also read 1 Peter 3:8,9 about unity and loving one another: "Finally, all of you, live in harmony with one another; be sympathetic, love as brothers, be compassionate and humble. Do not repay evil for evil or insult with insult, but with blessing, because to this you were called." Then I prayed, "God, you are so awesome. You have truly been my strength through this whole process. You have shown me how to cast my cares upon You, and how to download whatever I need from heaven. I think I am only now realizing the journey I have been on. You have drop-shipped friends, money, wisdom, hugs, spa treatments, blueberry lemonade toasts, a shot of joy with my nieces and Mom, and prayer support. I ask You to save the best for last and let Mom's going be like the Fourth of July. Let there be fireworks in a wonderful way. Please bring reconciliation to my family—fully. I believe there are still a few more shots to be launched from Mom."

I thought about some ladies who Calene and I had met at the Pinehurst Hotel during her visit. They were sisters talking about their mom's death. Since she loved cocktail hour, all the children would meet at the house at 5 p.m. and have cocktail hour with her. During her last few days, they stayed with her, and on her last night they call crawled in bed with her and slept with her. It was so beautiful. The entire family was there to show their support. They agreed to be nice to one another in front of their mother, regardless of how they felt otherwise. One daughter moved in with her mother for four months, leaving her job. How remarkable. Funny, they were talking about death and the place of faith. They weren't certain of their salvation, but thought it was better to believe than not to.

That afternoon, I lay in bed with Mom. We had a few chuckles. She shared some private thoughts with me that made me realize what God was doing to wrap things up for her in these last days of her life and to reconcile some things in the family.

On the way home, I lost it. The finality of Mom's life hit me hard. I thought about how seven years ago God had turned my heart toward Mom and told me to focus on her. I didn't know why, but He showed me saying, "Because you are preparing her for death." I never knew just how important the end of life is to God, but it is. And I was a faithful daughter to obey God and prepare His handmaiden, my mother, to meet her Maker.

I was hit with the emotions that came with knowing her time had finally come. I called Melissa, my friend and spiritual sister who lives in Virginia. She broke down and cried when I told her the salute and rose story. We laughed and prayed.

I went over to Sarah's, my neighbor across the street, and asked for a hug. I didn't know her all that well, but she was emotionally available and fully supportive of my situation with Mom. She confessed that she'd had a fallout with her father. There is need for reconciliation everywhere. God, do your thing.

On Friday, December 21, 2007, Mom had her final visit from our mutual friend, Peggy, who had played golf with us the first time Mom teed it up at Pine Needles. Peggy could read me emotionally better than anyone I've ever known. She gave me the gift of her presence and support as she jumped in her car on Friday morning and drove all the way to Fayetteville from Virginia Beach, a half day trip, to spend just a few hours with Mom and me—and then drove all the way back to Virginia that evening.

When Peggy came, the hospice nurse was finishing up with Mom. Peggy brought some beautiful flowers to add to the roses that were already there. The roses were opening up to full bloom—every one of them. Peggy loved on Mom—they had such a domestic connection. What I remember most is Mom and Peggy talking about the green pepper plant Mom had growing in the spare bedroom. There was one little pepper hanging like a charm. Mom was so proud of it.

Friday was also the day Mom's hospital bed was delivered. Peggy and I put her sheets on and after a good visit, decided to help her into bed. Mom lay down flat in the bed for a split second, and all of sudden everything changed. She began to have a terrible time breathing. Nancy came in and gave her some medication. It was scary. I had never seen Mom in that much pain and suffering. I knew her heart was shutting down. It was a big mistake to let her lie flat on the bed, even for a few moments. Her congestive heart failure took over.

When Peggy left, she said to me at the door, "Veronica, it's time. Your mom is ready to go home to be with Jesus." I wish I had taken her words to me more seriously. I didn't realize at the time that God had sent Peggy to me to tell me, "It is time!"

Later that night the lady with the oxygen unit came by. Mom was sleeping and I was stressed out trying to understand how to further help her. She was dying and the urgency of the moment was emotionally overwhelming for me.

Earlier, Mom asked me to spend the night with her. I raced home to grab my things and was thankful I made the trip to come back, as it turned out to be her last night.

Final Night and Day

Since she was sleeping in the chair, I crawled into the hospital bed next to her. At first I tried sleeping in the other room, but somehow I knew I needed to be beside her.

It was an amazing experience to be that close to Mom. These were the most intimate moments I'd ever shared with her—to spend the night when she was dying. It was also discomforting to see her fade in and out a hallucinogenic state. I remember lying in bed thinking, "This is just where I am supposed to be." I felt the peace that came from knowing I was in the perfect will of God.

About midnight she woke up, and said, "Veronica, what are you doing here?"

"You asked me to be here, Mom!"

"Oh." Did you see those big red lines that just shot across the room?" In one breath she was lucid; in another, she was in another world. We slept, chatted, and breathed next to one another until 4:30 when she awoke and wanted to vomit.

I helped her to the bathroom. She didn't vomit, but was having a tough time. I knew at that time that she was holding on by a thread. She declined the offer to have her regular breakfast of oatmeal. Instead, I gave her a muffin and a small glass of orange juice.

We sat and talked until later that morning when the dog agility show came on TV. We watched each dog go through the course. After each one, we said to each other, "Teddy would be faster!"

Suddenly, Mom blurted out, "Oh, did you see that big purple flower blow up? Veronica, the drawer is on fire. Put out the fire!"

"Mom, you don't even have to go to the movies! You can just close your eyes and see all kinds of action!" We laughed, but I knew this was serious.

Mom wanted to be sure that Samantha, the little girl who lived across the street from her, got her last five dollars. She went into her purse and emptied out all that she had. "Here, give this to Samantha for Christmas. She'll like this."

Later that morning we spoke about heaven. I told her that in heaven there is no more sorrow—no tears, pain, or sickness. There are streets of gold. She seemed to like that idea. I read her Scriptures. One said, "Wherever there is breath, praise the Lord."

She said with me, "Praise the Lord."

Around 11:00 a.m., I needed to leave to go back and get Teddy. I had left him at the neighbor's to stay the night so I could be with Mom. "Mom," I said, "I'm really worn out. Maybe I'll take a day off and visit you on Monday. That means you will need to be around for two more days. Can you say that with me?"

She replied, "I will stay around for two more days." In my spiritual gut, I knew that might not be possible.

Later that afternoon, I was in great turmoil about leaving her. Something kept saying, "Stay with her." I called Peggy. "What do you think?"

"You need to be with your Mom," she said without hesitation.

Pastor Hedgepeth, my brother's pastor and my long-time friend, called and exhorted me to relax. He assured me, "Everything will work out all right." I didn't know what to do. I wanted to be there, but I was also worn out from the stress.

I called Mom about 6 p.m. She seemed to be quite alert after Nancy gave her a breathing treatment. The question that came to mind, however, was, "I wonder how long this is going to last." About 8:00 I was in Staples, putting together the calendar for her Christmas present to everyone. Something said to me, "What are you doing here? You need to be with your mother." I was struggling greatly with the whole notion of going back over to my brother's. I thought, "If she's is doing that badly, they would call me." I should have listened to my gut.

And they did. At 11:00 I got a call that Mom was having terrible problems breathing; it appeared that this was it. I jumped in my car and drove over to her apartment, racing about 100 miles an hour. My heart was racing even faster. I never thought I would be apart from her as she drew her final breath. I called Mike and asked him to put the cell phone next to her ear. "Hang on, Mom, until I get there. Hang on. Don't go until I get there. I love you." I made that call about three times. The fourth time the phone was busy, an ominous sign.

I arrived about fifteen minutes too late. Mom had died in the arms of my brother and sister-in-law. Nancy said it was probably good that I wasn't there because it wasn't a pretty site. Mom was screaming out to Jesus to take her. After a great struggle, she became peaceful and then went home to be with the Lord. I prayed for over twenty years to be there when Mom passed. It didn't happen.

When I came into her bedroom, she was lying flat on the bed, with eyes slightly open, hands folded, and her mouth open. It was surreal, because she looked like she was still alive. I kissed her on the forehead and said, "I love you, Mom." Surprisingly, I didn't lose it. I was amazed to feel so calm.

Pastor Hedgepeth got there shortly thereafter and consoled us all as we spoke about the details of a memorial service. His manner was very soothing. There was peace in the room. It as if all the warfare had lifted. My family invited me to spend the night. I just wanted to sleep in my own bed back home in Pinehurst.

I got into bed at about 2:00 a.m. and knew I had to go to church the next day. My strength has always been in the Lord, and I knew the service would provide a shot of that strength, so I drove back to Fayetteville early the next morning.

During the service at Northwood, I became very emotional. The pastor mentioned Mom's passing from the pulpit. I started to cry. From across the sanctuary, Chuck Eplar, the head of the Sunday school class, came over to me. He drew me aside and gave me the most wonderful embrace. It was as if he were impressing his spirit on me, giving me strength in my weakness. It was beautiful. After holding me for a few minutes, he whispered in my ear, "I love you." It was an amazing moment. In some mysterious way, it was as if his voice was my mother's voice saying, "I love you," along with God's voice and his own. I will never forget that moment of finding strength, love, and acceptance in the presence of God in the house of the Lord. Many people came over to me after the service to hug me. It was the best place to be for someone who had no one to hold her.

I wasn't sure what to do after the service, but Chuck encouraged me to go by my family's house, visit them, and build on their invitation of the night before. It was a brief but pleasant visit. "What are you doing for Christmas?" Mike asked.

"I'd like to go to the Christmas Eve service at Northwood."

"Would you like to spend the night?" he asked. I welcomed the invitation.

So I went and enjoyed a pleasant dinner with family. Then Nancy, Rachel, Elise and I played a card game called Phase 10. It was nice because it wasn't mentally challenging and provided an easy way for us to socialize. We ended up talking about the last night of Mom's life, about the events that led up to her final moments and the timing of my trip. It was hard for me to process not being there for Mom's death. I had longed to see her all the way through to her last breath, but it wasn't meant to be. Would things have been different if I had listened to my own spirit and been there for Mom on her last night? Was it better for me that I wasn't there to witness the pain she went through? Was it meant to be for only my brother's family to be there so they could have those moments to share together? I don't know. Perhaps Nancy was right in telling me I was better off not seeing Mom's terrible suffering at the end. Perhaps God spared me by allowing me to remember her as she was for the better part of the day when I was last with her. But even so, this was my mother, and I had wanted to be there when her spirit departed to be with the Lord.

We spoke about a lot of things. Someone brought up how Mom enjoyed a cup of peppermint ice cream. Nancy offered me the last scoop in her honor. Rachel consoled me. "Aunt Dee, I know it will be really hard for you to be without Grandma, but she's in a better place." Elise kept giving me the skip card in the card game, which meant that I had to skip my turn, and we laughed about how many times that happened. It was a good way to process a very difficult night. My family appeared to be pretty unemotional about Mom's death, and in some strange way, their lack of emotion helped give me some balance.

It was the best time I had ever spent with them. Somehow I had to believe that Mom had the final shot of joy. She decided to go home with the Lord at a time when it would be natural to get together with my family—right at Christmas.

That morning we opened presents. Rachel and Elise paid special attention to the gifts they had all bought me: two pairs of socks, a nice candle, a special storage box for my Christmas ornaments, a Smoothie maker, and fifty dollars from my brother. I waited until all the presents were opened before giving the gifts from Grandma.

It was strange, but somehow appropriate. I gave them each a calendar with pictures of Mom on each month's page. Then I gave them money and gift certificates. I thought it would be nice to give them gift certificates from my friend's gift shop so they could buy something that would remind them of Mom.

When Mike found out that I didn't have a digital camera, he left the room and came back with a box. I opened it to find a brand new digital camera. I was touched. Then, without my even asking, he packed my car with all my stuff. We went over the flow of Mom's memorial service together and picked out pictures. It went really well. It was a bit hard to be in Mom's apartment, but I managed okay. We went through her safety box together. In it was a letter from her. I thought I was going to be a big "you are wonderful letter," but it turned out to be a list of all her possessions in the apartment, and how she left it all to me. She even told me what to do with some of the things. Still directing me!

I went back to Pinehurst that Christmas Day, and when I got home, turned on the lights of my tree. Reflecting on the events of the past twenty-four hours, I wrote in my journal, "Tonight as I watch the lights on my Christmas tree sparkle and shine, I feel the peace and love of God. It is a miracle. My heart is full. I can't imagine what it would be like to experience death at a time other than Christmas, but to experience death during this beautiful season is an amazing thing. Impressed upon the spirit of sadness, grief, loss, and pain is joy, fullness, celebration, connection, family, hospitality, and life. I believe God arranged Mom to go home with Him at the perfect moment for me to connect to His love at Christmas, to the Body of Christ, to my family. I don't think we would have had this next natural step without Christmas occurring right after Mom left us to be with Jesus. Thank you, God!"

Comfort and Joy

*T*he week following Mom's death was filled with preparations for her funeral service. She wanted to be cremated, so we agreed to have a memorial service in her honor at Northwood Temple in Fayetteville.

Back in the fall, I had a two-by-three-foot picture made of Mom smelling roses in the Duke Gardens. My friend Troy had taken the unposed picture of Mom doing her thing. It truly was a God moment. The florist made a beautiful arrangement around the picture.

All week long I kept getting phone calls and expressions of love and support from people. I am loved! Loved by God and others. The greatest blessing was my friend Janet, who came in from Michigan just to support me. The year before, God had impressed it upon her heart to be with me when this time came. True to her word, she came Friday noon and went home Sunday evening. She did everything, from buying me groceries, cooking dinner, helping me tweek my eulogy, counseling me, praying for me, encouraging me, and supporting me during the memorial service. Most significant of all, she went back to Mom's apartment with me after the service to pack up her things.

I bought a new outfit for the funeral. I had planned to wear my standard old black pants that make me look thin. When I put them on, however, I noticed the zipper was broken. It was the first time I realized Mom was gone when I said to myself, "Oh, no. My zipper is broken, and Mom isn't here to fix it!" So, I bought a new pair of slacks. I found them at the first store I visited in the Village of Pinehurst. They fit perfectly. Janet treated me to a new blouse at Talbots. I asked Mike to bring me Mom's iridescent blue earrings, the same ones in the picture, to wear in her honor.

The last command Mom had given me was to get my hair cut. Because I was running around nonstop the day before the service, I couldn't make it the hair salon until 5:00 that evening. I explained my plight to Melodie, the owner, and she gladly worked me in for a good hair trim. She even gave me some rollers to use in my hair for the next morning.

The memorial service went fine. The pastor gave a compelling message that focused on the human spirit and emphasized the need for one to be certain of knowing where they're going. As a result of his message, several people found salvation as they placed their faith in God. We sang "Amazing Grace," "The Lord's Prayer, and "Silent Night." The pastor led communion and spoke about Mom. I was impressed with how he pegged her to a tee, even though he had not known her very well. He spoke of her as a woman on a journey, a Catholic, a fighter, and feisty woman.

Several friends came down from Virginia Beach who knew Mom and me, including Calene and her family. It was wonderful to have true friends there, people who loved Mom. However, I was disappointed that not a single family member came outside of the immediate family. Lunch afterward was also a meaningful time.

People got up to share stories about Mom. Maarten, Calene's husband, told one about her love for beer. In fact, several funny stories about beer were related. Then Nancy shared, and I shared. It was a good time of fellowship.

Even though I wasn't present for Mom's passing, Nancy told me a story that made me realize how one in the spirit we were with each other: "About 9:00 p.m., just a few hours before your mom died, she somehow found enough strength to get up out of bed and straggle to the refrigerator. She was looking for a beer and actually had taken a gulp by the time we got there and helped her back to bed. 'I'm thirsty, and wanted a good beer,' she said."

"No way," I said to Nancy. "At the same time Mom was looking for a beer, I opened up my refrigerator in my kitchen, at home in Pinehurst, some sixty miles away. I looked inside and found a Michelob Light. I said to myself, 'Mom loves beer. I'm going over there tomorrow, and I'm going to bring her this can of beer.' I set it on my kitchen counter. To think that Mom and I were both reaching for a can of beer at the same time! I guess she was celebrating her home-going and wanted to say, 'Here's to ya. I'm outta here!' I took it as a confirmation of the deep connection of spirit we shared in her final moments."

A Profound Truth

*S*hortly after Mom's funeral, I was home by myself. I suddenly had a great sense of my aloneness. One of the hardest periods of loss is not the time leading up to a loved one's death, but immediately following. There was no one to be with me once I returned home. I was sitting one morning in utter silence in my living room, being as still as I could possibly could, when the Lord spoke a powerful and clear word to my heart and mind: "Your mother is not dead. She's just not with you. She is more alive than you are right now."

Those words helped me to process, at least in part, the pain and anger I still felt for not being there when she died. I had beaten myself up a thousand times over this. Perhaps God allowed me to be absent in order for Him to reveal a more profound and eternal truth—Mom lives on. I was there for her in her life—and she is now leaping for joy in heaven, alive as alive can be. To meditate on this eternal truth helped to lift from me any spirit of grief and anger that could have overwhelmed me.

A few days later, I was being still again, just soaking in the peace and utter aloneness of the moment, not rejecting it, but allowing it to be. Another profound truth hit me as I read a Scripture passage from 1 Thessalonians 5:10: "He died for us so that, whether we are awake or asleep, we may live together with him." What this verse revealed to me was that Mom was still with me. Because of Christ, she had not left me. She was simply "over there" as I was "over here," but we were still together in Christ. It didn't matter that she was asleep and I was awake. We could come together through Christ.

Although this was a total mystery to me, the thought that I was still with Mom and she with me was a great comfort.

More than any other time in my life, I came to comprehend the great reality of salvation. To many people salvation is just a cosmic notion out in the sweet by and by. When a loved one dies, however, the central truth of the Christian faith—the resurrection—becomes a practical reality. Death is swallowed up in victory! Because Jesus Christ rose from the dead, the sorrow and pain I would feel from death is elevated to a fresh hope of eternal life. Knowing I will see Mom again kept my spirit elevated and has brought much comfort to me.

Because I adopted a listening ear throughout the last leg of Mom's journey to heaven, God revealed to me secrets from on high that kept me from falling into the pits. While I had to go through a process of grief recovery, I never experienced a spirit of grief. In fact, I also came to realize that the opposite of grief is honor. When you truly honor someone, it keeps their memory alive, and the relationship alive. All the ways that I honored my mother became a form of sowing forward. After her death, I reaped incredible joy each time I told some of our stories and adventures, a joy that replaced grief. I didn't expect this, but God so honored my investment with my mother that He paid me off on this end with a fullness in my heart that is truly eternal.

As I was processing the intense reality of my loss, I got a call from Bonnie McGowan one morning. Bonnie is the daughter of golfing great, Peggy Kirk Bell. When I played college golf for Duke, Bonnie played for the University of North Carolina. Her words comforted me: "Veronica, when my father passed away many years ago, I was determined to keep his memory alive. As unusual as this sounds, I have communicated with his spirit over the years, and often remember him."

Her words rang true to me. Later that day, I was driving down the road, thinking about that perfect day we had back in early December at the Reindeer Fun Run. It was not only a perfect day, but the last normal day I had with my mom. I thought about the amazing journey that transpired and the many transformations that took place over the seven years prior to that day in order for perfection to become a reality. As I reflected on our race together, I looked at the car in front of me. The license plate read, "Race on!" My entire eulogy had been about Mom running a race. The Reindeer Fun Run was about running a race. I couldn't help but think that Mom was already peeking over the yellow ropes of heaven, cheering me on. "Run your race, Veronica. Keep going. It's time for you now. Go, baby, go!" She was handing off the baton to me.

So I reached up, grabbed it, and winked up at her, knowing that that perfect day with my mother would live on forever. The real perfection was not in the events of the day but in the love that was worked out in my heart for Mom and others, an unconditional love from God that also made me whole. I have come to realize that love means entering someone else's world. I entered my mother's world of pain, illness, and elderliness. She entered my world of golf and speaking. We entered one another's world of athleticism. That perfect day, I entered her world, which will forever remind me of who she was, what her life was all about, and what we shared. It will remind me of her beauty and strength and undaunted faith all the way to the finish line.

I reached out to my mother, and it was through her that I found myself. I believe my whole life has been a quest to find a relationship with my parents. Now that I have completed that journey of reconciliation, I can run my own race, live my own life, and carry with me the joy of knowing my mother forever.

I entered the championship and, by God's grace, won the ultimate challenge to love.

Epilogue

*A*s I put the finishing touches on this book, I'm sitting on the lovely big porch at the Carolina Hotel in Pinehurst. There are so many things I love about Pinehurst, especially this hotel, but one of them is the porch. A porch is a place where people who know one another and those who don't can meet, talk, and connect. It's a casual but intimate place. Rocking chairs and big green ferns line the long outside hallway. The fans blow as resort guests walk by. A man stops to blow on his cigar. Two businessmen gather to talk through a proposal. Resort workers talk about setting up an activity. But the best thing about this porch is the beautiful view. You can sit here, have an engaging conversation with someone, or simply share silent moments to look out onto the colorful flowers and kids splashing in the pool. It's a place where you can quiet yourself and just be.

I learned from my journey with Mom that we all need porches in our lives—places and platforms where we can come outside of ourselves and meet others with no expectation of changing them, just reaching out and being with them in a safe emotional place.

Mom and I found the porches in our lives—the golf course, the podium, our back porch, some mutual friends, the breakfast table, a vacation spot, our dog, and shopping. I found a way to make one connection at a time with her through my shots of joy strategy. And now I have the blessing of holding cherished memories of Mom in my heart.

I stopped at a yard sale on my way to the hotel to finish my writing. The nice lady having the sale helped bring my things to the car. We started talking about our mothers. Hers had just recently died. I began to share the story of reconciliation with my mother. "That's a beautiful story, Veronica, and makes me want to cry," she said. And she did.

Somewhere in the heart of every person is the deep desire and need for reconciliation with those from whom we're alienated. My friendship with Mom didn't begin with a complete overhaul of our relationship. It began with one connection at a time, with a resolve to reach her despite the cost.

One invitation at a time, to meet on a porch, a point of common interest, to rock on a rocking chair together, look out on a lovely view together, and enjoy one another's company. The little connections are the big win.

Find your porch. Make your invitation. Take your shot. Do it now, because when they're gone, they're gone.

If I speak in the tongues of men or of angels, but do not have love, I am only a resounding gong or a clanging cymbal. If I have the gift of prophecy and can fathom all mysteries and all knowledge, and if I have a faith that can move mountains, but do not have love, I am nothing. If I give all I possess to the poor and give over my body to hardship that I may boast, but do not have love, I gain nothing. Love is patient, love is kind. It does not envy, it does not boast, it is not proud. It does not dishonor others, it is not self-seeking, it is not easily angered, it keeps no record of wrongs. Love does not delight in evil but rejoices with the truth. It always protects, always trusts, always hopes, always perseveres. Love never fails... And now these three remain: faith, hope and love. But the greatest of these is love. (1Corinthians 13:1-8a, 13)

Appendix 1

How to Create Your Own Shot of Joy

*T*he game of golf offers powerful analogies for relationships that work to bring about transformation. You certainly do not have to be a golfer to take advantage of the applied lessons. All you have to do is understand the truths and then create your own shot of joy. The good news is, you can hit as many shots as you need to until you hit it on the sweet spot!

The following are analogies from the game that form principles and approaches for relationship transformation:

1. Golf is series of shots that you hit one at a time. Like golf, relationships are made and transformed by making one relational connection at a time. Most people look at a difficult relationship and think it can't be changed because they are focusing on the whole relationship. If you just focus on making one shot—one relational connection—you have a better chance at seeing change.

2. Hitting shots is intentional. The best players "call their shots" before they hit them. For example, a pro might say, "I'm going to hit a slight fade around this tree and play it safe to the middle of the green." The best relational connections are also made by being intentional. That means you have to decide what you want your shot to look like. You can't be passive. What kind of connection do you want to make with your challenging loved one? Most people would simply like a real conversation or a real memory. You can create a great memory without reconciling the entire relationship.

3. To make a good shot, invoke your imagination and visualize your shot. The best shots in golf are hit from the most impossible lies. Ever see Tiger Woods caught behind a tree with his ball lying deep in the rough? Next thing you know, he hits a great shot and it lands right next to the pin. (Well, at least he *used* to hit those shots!) How did he do that? He invoked the power of his imagination to see the shot before he hit it. Forget the mechanics of your conflict for a second. Instead, take a minute and imagine what you want your relational connection to look like. Where will you meet? For how long? What will you be doing? What emotional resolve will you have to make to execute the shot? Do you need to give the person a heads up about your intent before you meet? The greatest power you have is the power to create.

4. Choose the right atmosphere in which to hit your shots. I've always played my best games in a positive, fun atmosphere playing with my most enjoyable golf buddies. We cut up, tease one another, and evoke a positive emotional space to swing free. In relationships, there is always at least one positive meeting place of common interest where people enjoy one another's company. Where do you experience a positive connection with your challenging loved one? In cooking together, shooting hoops, fishing, playing card games? In what scenario is it easy for the other person to engage with you? Find it and go there. You can't change a person, but you can change the atmosphere.

5. Hit the shot! If you don't have the courage to hit the shot, you will never know what the possible outcome can be. To hit a shot of joy, have the courage to set up your shot, execute it, and then let go of the need to control the outcome. Just release the shot and see where it lands. If it doesn't land where you intended it to go, put another ball down and hit it again!

In the years following my shot of joy with my mother, I've helped many people set up their own shots of joy with difficult loved ones. Here's just one example: Charli was dreading to see her family over the holidays. She loved her mother but was at odds with her stepfather. She needed a shot of joy. I asked her, "What is it that you want from your visit?"

After we talked it through and identified her truest feelings, she said, "I want a fresh connection with my mother. I missed her birthday and we've been not as close lately."

"What would your shot look like?" I asked.

"I'd like to have my siblings gather around Mom with me to give her a gift and spend a few minutes together sharing privately."

"What kind of gift would create a great connection?"

She replied, "When we were growing up we had these red and white checked shirts. We had the best memories of our family all wearing those same shirts. Recently, I was in Israel and bought some beautiful necklaces for everyone. My ideal plan is that I would tell the story of our red and white shirts and how they represented our family's intimacy. Then I want to give the necklaces as a present-day expression of renewal of that same intimacy."

"Great!" I said. Now let's set up your shot. I directed her to call her mother ahead of time, and to tell her she wanted to get together with her and her siblings for twenty minutes before the family dinner to share something special. Charli made the call, and her mother agreed to the gathering. Charli executed her shot perfectly! It created a fresh, intimate connection with her mother and sisters—and created a cherished memory for years to come.

Here is an easy way to remember how to set up a shot with the 5 R's:

1. **Reframe:** You can't change a person, but you can change the atmosphere. Set you mind to do so. What do you want to change? What don't you want anymore?
2. **Reflect:** Decide on what a successful/meaningful experience would look like. Visualize it. What is the new outcome you would like to have? In what scenarios does your family/loved one positively engage? What would warm your heart? What do

you want? What is your desire? How can you engage them to create your desired outcome?

3. **Release:** Dump your own junk. Forgive and wipe the slate clean before you start. Your shot of joy has to start from a clean, calm place in your own heart. What do you need to forgive them for before you see them? What disempowering emotion do you need to replace with an empowering one?

4. **Resolve:** Commit ahead of time with regard to how you will respond to negativity. Refuse to be offended. Keep the battle on the outside. Set your boundaries. It's the spirit working through the person, not the person who is the enemy. What does the boundary look like: physical distance, time, place, an activity? It's okay to set your boundary without feeling guilty. Just be authentic and realistic.

5. **Recreate:** You have the power to change the energy. What would a shot of joy look like? Where do you naturally experience positive energy with your loved one? What are you shared interests? What action steps will you take to make it happen without controlling the outcome? What kind of invitation can you make that will make it comfortable for the other person to respond to?

Unlike golf, where you forget most of your shots, you will never forget hitting your shots of joy. So go ahead and tee it up. The best shots come from the most impossible lies.

Appendix II

*R*eview of Relationship-Building Dynamics from *My Shot of Joy*:

1. Every great championship begins with a resolve to win. What is your resolve going to be with regard to redeeming your lost relationship?
2. Go to God and ask Him for a Scripture as a confirmation and "biblical swing-thought" upon which to activate your faith.
3. Continue to pray throughout and ask the Holy Spirit to reveal things to you and guide you through the transformational process.
4. Your loved one can never give you what was lost in the past, so accept the loss and quit demanding they give you something that no longer exists.
5. You cannot fix—or fill—the past, but you can start something brand new today.
6. Deal with your own heart first.
7. Stand back "emotionally" and just begin to observe the other person....what makes them tick.
8. You cannot change a person, but you can change the atmosphere. In what atmospheres is it easy and natural for you both to connect? This is what I experienced with Mom as being "in the diamonds," where you connect spirit to spirit. Most often it is within a common interest.
9. Don't be overwhelmed or stuck with looking at the entire relationship. Just make one relational connection at a time.

10. Set up your shot strategically. Think through what you want to create, what the invitation looks like, and what outcome you desire. Think through what would make it easy for the other person to respond to.

11. Use words that are generative. In other words, use language that expresses what you want, not what the current story is. "I want a fresh start with you" are powerful words that many have used with great success.

12. Let go of the outcome. Don't try to control it. Set up your shot and wherever it lands is where it lands. Give the other person complete freedom to respond however he/she desires.

13. Hit the shot! If you don't ever hit it, you'll never know what is possible.

14. Transformation begins with you. You don't have to wait for the other person to change to enter into a new dimension with her. If you change the way you relate to the person, she will have the opportunity to change the way she relates to you.

15. Connecting to another person is not a matter of chemistry or personality, but of using the right building blocks of relationships.

16. If you want to truly reconcile with someone, stop trying to be right and start working on reaching the person's heart.

17. There is always an angle to reach someone. You have to be patient and keep sending shots of joy to discover what the open angle is.

18. The greatest power you have is the power to create.

19. If you want to experience something new, you have to do something new!

20. Focus on improving your conversations, because the conversation is the relationship. No conversation = no relationship.

If you have a story of how a shot of joy relationship dynamic has
Helped or improved a relationship, I would love to hear from you.
Please contact me at: veronica@truechampioncoaching.com.

If you would like to see a video of Mom hitting a golf ball and
a 2 minute powerpoint story of her journey, visit:
www.truechampioncoaching.com/milly

For speaking engagements, contact Veronica at
www.truechampioncoaching.com
www.facebook.com/Veronica Karaman Coaching

Also by Veronica Karaman:

A Quiet Clap: Life Lessons Appreciating God and Golf

God's Way to an A.com/Class

The Spirit-led Student: My Journey Out of Performance and Into His Presence

Made in the USA
Middletown, DE
06 June 2016